Gator Grit

Gator Grit

Matthew Petchinsky

1

Gator Grit: Harnessing the Power of Resilience in Tough Times

By: Matthew Petchinsky

Disclaimer

This book, *Gator Grit: Harnessing the Power of Resilience in Tough Times*, is intended for educational, motivational, and informational purposes only. It is designed to offer perspectives, strategies, and reflections on resilience, personal strength, and navigating adversity. While every effort has been made to present thoughtful and practical guidance, this book does not constitute professional advice of any kind, including but not limited to medical, psychological, psychiatric, legal, or financial advice. Readers are encouraged to seek qualified professionals for support tailored to their individual circumstances.

The concepts, techniques, and strategies discussed within this book are based on general principles of personal development, mindset training, and resilience-building. Results may vary significantly from person to person depending on individual effort, life circumstances, health conditions, and external factors beyond the author's control. The author and publisher make no guarantees regarding specific outcomes, including financial success, emotional healing, physical endurance, or life transformation.

This book may explore themes related to stress, hardship, trauma, survival, and personal struggle. While these topics are approached with the intention of empowerment and growth, they may be triggering or emotionally intense for some readers. If you are experiencing severe emotional distress, mental health challenges, or crisis situations, it is strongly recommended that you seek immediate assistance from a licensed mental health professional, medical provider, or appropriate emergency services.

Any references to physical activity, endurance, outdoor survival, or lifestyle changes are presented for general informational purposes only. Readers should consult a qualified healthcare provider before engaging in any new physical, dietary, or lifestyle practices, especially if they have pre-existing health conditions or concerns. The author and publisher are not responsible for any injuries, health complications, or damages that may result from the application of the information contained in this book.

This book may include anecdotes, metaphors, or illustrative examples inspired by real-life situations or symbolic storytelling. These are intended solely for educational and motivational purposes and should not be interpreted as literal advice or guarantees. Any resemblance to actual persons, living or dead, or real events is purely coincidental unless otherwise stated.

The reader assumes full responsibility for their actions, decisions, and results after engaging with this material. By reading this book, you acknowledge that you are using your own judgment and discretion in applying any ideas, strategies, or practices presented. The author and publisher disclaim any liability for direct, indirect, incidental, or consequential damages arising from the use or misuse of the information provided.

This work is not affiliated with, endorsed by, or connected to any governmental, wildlife, or environmental agency. Any references to animals, including alligators or other wildlife, are symbolic, metaphorical, or educational in nature and are not intended to encourage unsafe interactions with wildlife or the environment.

Finally, this book is a tool—not a guarantee. Resilience is a deeply personal and evolving process shaped by time, effort, support systems, and lived experience. The purpose of *Gator Grit* is to offer guidance, perspective, and strength along the way, but the path forward ultimately belongs to you.

Introduction: What is Gator Grit? The Power of Resilience

There's a certain kind of strength that doesn't announce itself. It doesn't need applause, validation, or permission. It doesn't break under pressure—it adapts, endures, and waits for the right moment to move. That strength is what this book calls *Gator Grit.*

Gator Grit is not about being loud, aggressive, or invincible. It's about being unshakable in a world that constantly tries to shake you. It is the quiet, relentless force inside you that keeps going when everything else says stop. It is the ability to survive harsh environments, recover from setbacks, and come back stronger—not because life got easier, but because you got tougher.

Think about the alligator—not as an animal to imitate physically, but as a symbol of raw, grounded resilience. It has existed for millions of years, surviving extreme changes in climate, terrain, and threat. It doesn't waste energy. It doesn't panic. It observes, adapts, and strikes only when necessary. It thrives in environments that would break most creatures. That is the essence of Gator Grit.

This book is built on that principle: you don't need perfect conditions to thrive. You need the ability to endure imperfect ones.

Resilience is often misunderstood. People think it means pushing through pain without rest, pretending everything is fine, or never feeling fear. That's not resilience—that's suppression. Real resilience is much deeper. It's the ability to feel everything—fear, frustration, exhaustion—and still choose to move forward anyway. It's not about avoiding the storm. It's about learning how to stand in it without losing yourself.

Gator Grit is resilience with awareness. It is strength with strategy. It is patience with purpose.

In tough times, most people look for quick escapes—distractions, shortcuts, or ways to numb the discomfort. But resilience isn't built in comfort. It's built in the moments where you don't have easy answers. It's forged in uncertainty, pressure, and repetition. It's developed when you decide—again and again—that quitting is not your default response.

This book does not promise an easy path. It does not offer shortcuts or illusions of overnight transformation. What it offers is something far more valuable: a framework for becoming the kind of person who can handle anything life throws at them.

Because here's the truth—life will test you.

There will be days when everything feels like it's working against you. Days where progress is invisible. Days where you question whether the effort is worth it. Gator Grit is what carries you through those days. It's the discipline to keep moving, the awareness to adjust your approach, and the patience to trust that growth is happening—even when you can't see it yet.

This concept applies to every area of life.

In finances, Gator Grit means rebuilding when everything collapses. It means staying disciplined when others give up. It's the mindset that turns scarcity into strategy.

In health, it means listening to your body while still committing to improvement. It's not about extremes—it's about consistency, even on your worst days.

In relationships, Gator Grit means setting boundaries, recognizing your worth, and refusing to stay in environments that drain you. It's the strength to walk away when necessary and the wisdom to stay and build when it matters.

In creativity, it's the ability to produce, create, and express—even when motivation is gone. Especially when motivation is gone.

You don't need to be perfect to have Gator Grit. You don't need to have everything figured out. You don't even need to feel ready.

You just need to be willing to stay in the game.

This book will guide you through the layers of resilience—mental, emotional, physical, and strategic. It will show you how to conserve your energy instead of wasting it, how to recognize when to act and when to wait, and how to build a mindset that doesn't collapse under pressure.

You will learn how to operate with intention instead of reaction. How to move with purpose instead of panic. How to develop a kind of inner stability that doesn't depend on external conditions.

Because once you build that—once you develop true Gator Grit—you become difficult to break.

Not because life stops being hard.

But because you've become stronger than the hard.

This is not about becoming someone else. It's about becoming the version of yourself that can endure, adapt, and rise—no matter what environment you're placed in.

You already have the foundation.

This book is here to sharpen it.

Chapter 1: Thick Skin: Learning to Withstand Life's Hardships

The Nature of Thick Skin

Thick skin is not about becoming cold or unfeeling. It is about developing the ability to endure pressure without losing your identity. Life will test you repeatedly, and without some form of emotional protection, those tests can wear you down over time. Thick skin acts as a buffer between your inner world and external chaos.

Most people mistake sensitivity for weakness, but that isn't entirely true. Sensitivity becomes a liability only when it is unmanaged. When you take every comment personally or allow every setback to define you, you give away your power. Thick skin allows you to feel without being controlled by those feelings.

Hardships are not random interruptions in life—they are part of the structure of growth. Every challenge you face is an opportunity to strengthen your resilience. The problem is not the hardship itself, but how you interpret and respond to it.

When you begin to see difficulties as training instead of punishment, your mindset shifts. You stop asking, "Why is this happening to me?" and start asking, "What is this teaching me?" That shift alone builds emotional endurance.

Thick skin develops through exposure, not avoidance. The more you face discomfort, the more familiar it becomes. Over time, what once felt overwhelming starts to feel manageable. This is how resilience is built—through repetition.

Avoiding hardship may feel safe in the moment, but it weakens you in the long run. Every time you avoid a challenge, you reinforce the belief that you cannot handle it. Thick skin is built by doing the opposite—by stepping into difficulty and proving to yourself that you can endure.

It's important to understand that thick skin doesn't mean ignoring pain. It means acknowledging it without letting it control your decisions. You can feel hurt and still move forward. You can feel fear and still act.

At its core, thick skin is about stability. It is the ability to remain grounded no matter what is happening around you. When you develop this, you become less reactive and more intentional in how you navigate life.

Emotional Armor Without Losing Yourself

One of the biggest dangers in building resilience is becoming emotionally shut down. There is a difference between being strong and being numb. Thick skin should protect you, not disconnect you from your humanity.

Emotional armor is meant to filter, not block. You still need to experience joy, connection, and meaning. If your defenses become too rigid, you risk isolating yourself from the very things that make life worth living.

Balance is key. You want to be strong enough to handle criticism, rejection, and failure without collapsing—but still open enough to receive love, growth, and opportunity. This balance is what defines true resilience.

When you build emotional armor correctly, you become selective about what you allow to affect you. Not everything deserves your energy. Not every opinion matters. Thick skin helps you distinguish between useful feedback and meaningless noise.

This selectivity gives you control. Instead of reacting to everything, you choose your responses. This is where power begins—when you stop being controlled by external forces and start directing your internal state.

It's also important to recognize that not all criticism is negative. Some of it is necessary for growth. Thick skin allows you to receive constructive feedback without taking it as a personal attack.

At the same time, it protects you from destructive criticism—comments meant to tear you down rather than build you up. Learning to tell the difference is a crucial part of developing resilience.

Ultimately, emotional armor should make you stronger, not smaller. It should expand your capacity to handle life, not limit your ability to experience it.

Facing Pressure Without Breaking

Pressure is one of life's most consistent forces. It shows up in finances, relationships, health, and personal growth. How you respond to pressure determines your trajectory.

Many people break under pressure because they resist it. They try to escape it, deny it, or fight it without understanding it. This resistance creates more stress and weakens their ability to cope.

Thick skin allows you to face pressure directly. Instead of avoiding it, you learn to stand in it. You recognize that pressure is not always an enemy—it can also be a catalyst for growth.

When you accept pressure as part of the process, it loses its power to overwhelm you. You stop seeing it as something to fear and start seeing it as something to navigate.

Adaptability is key. Pressure often requires you to adjust your approach. What worked before may not work now. Thick skin gives you the flexibility to change strategies without losing confidence.

It also helps you maintain focus. Under pressure, it's easy to become distracted or reactive. Thick skin keeps you grounded, allowing you to make clear, intentional decisions.

Over time, your tolerance for pressure increases. Situations that once felt unbearable become manageable. This is how you build endurance—not by avoiding pressure, but by learning to operate within it.

Eventually, you reach a point where pressure no longer controls you. You control how you respond to it. That is true resilience.

Detachment from External Validation

One of the fastest ways to weaken yourself is by relying on external validation. When your sense of worth depends on others' opinions, you become vulnerable to their approval or disapproval.

Thick skin requires a shift inward. Your validation must come from your own standards, your own effort, and your own growth. This doesn't mean ignoring others completely, but it does mean not depending on them.

When you detach from external validation, you gain freedom. You no longer need permission to act, create, or pursue your goals. You operate from internal confidence rather than external approval.

This shift also reduces emotional volatility. Praise doesn't inflate you, and criticism doesn't destroy you. You remain steady regardless of outside feedback.

It's important to recognize that not everyone will understand your path. Some people will doubt you, question you, or even try to discourage you. Thick skin allows you to continue anyway.

You begin to measure success differently. Instead of seeking approval, you focus on progress. You track your own growth rather than comparing yourself to others.

This internal focus builds long-term resilience. External validation is temporary and unreliable. Internal validation is stable and sustainable.

When you rely on yourself for validation, you become harder to shake. Your confidence is no longer tied to circumstances—it is rooted in your own sense of purpose.

Turning Pain into Power

Pain is unavoidable. Everyone experiences it in different forms—loss, failure, rejection, hardship. The question is not whether you will experience pain, but what you will do with it.

Thick skin allows you to process pain without being consumed by it. Instead of letting it weaken you, you use it as fuel for growth.

Every difficult experience carries a lesson. The more you reflect on those experiences, the more you extract value from them. Pain becomes a teacher rather than an obstacle.

This doesn't mean romanticizing suffering. It means recognizing that growth often comes through challenge. Avoiding pain entirely is not realistic, but learning from it is.

Resilience transforms pain into strength. Each hardship you overcome adds to your capacity. You become more capable, more aware, and more prepared for future challenges.

It also builds confidence. When you survive difficult situations, you prove to yourself that you can handle adversity. This belief becomes a foundation for future resilience.

Over time, your relationship with pain changes. You no longer fear it in the same way. You understand that while it may be uncomfortable, it is also temporary and often necessary for growth.

Pain, when used correctly, becomes a source of power. It shapes you into someone who can endure and evolve.

Consistency: The True Builder of Strength

Resilience is not built in a single moment. It is built through consistent action over time. Small, repeated efforts create lasting strength.

Many people look for quick transformations, but real change is gradual. Thick skin develops through daily practice—facing challenges, managing emotions, and staying committed.

Consistency builds trust in yourself. Every time you follow through, you reinforce the belief that you can rely on yourself. This trust is essential for resilience.

It also reduces fear. When you consistently face challenges, they become less intimidating. Familiarity replaces uncertainty, and confidence grows.

Discipline plays a major role. Even when you don't feel motivated, consistency keeps you moving forward. This is where true strength is developed.

Over time, these small actions compound. What once required effort becomes second nature. Resilience becomes part of who you are, not something you have to think about.

Consistency also creates stability. In a chaotic world, your habits become your anchor. They keep you grounded regardless of external circumstances.

Ultimately, thick skin is not a trait you are born with—it is a skill you build. And like any skill, it requires practice, patience, and persistence.

Alligator's Advice

The alligator does not rush. It watches, waits, and understands its environment before making a move. You don't need to react to everything immediately. Sometimes strength is found in patience, in observing before acting.

It conserves energy. It does not waste effort on unnecessary battles. Learn to choose your fights wisely. Not everything deserves your attention, and not every challenge requires an immediate response.

It survives harsh conditions by adapting, not resisting. When life changes, you must change with it. Stubbornness can break you, but adaptability keeps you alive and moving forward.

And when the moment comes, it acts with precision. No hesitation, no doubt. When you decide to move, do so with confidence. Trust your preparation, trust your instincts, and follow through.

Exercise 1: The Pressure Exposure Drill

Step 1: Identify one situation you have been avoiding due to discomfort or fear.

Step 2: Break it down into smaller, manageable actions.

Step 3: Commit to taking the first step within 24 hours.

Step 4: Reflect on how it felt and what you learned.

Step 5: Repeat the process, gradually increasing the level of challenge.

Exercise 2: Emotional Detachment Practice

Step 1: Think of a recent situation where you reacted emotionally.

Step 2: Write down what triggered your reaction.

Step 3: Ask yourself if the reaction was helpful or harmful.

Step 4: Reframe the situation with a more balanced perspective.

Step 5: Practice responding differently in similar future situations.

Exercise 3: Consistency Builder Routine

Step 1: Choose one small habit that supports resilience (e.g., journaling, exercise, reflection).

Step 2: Commit to doing it daily for 7 days.

Step 3: Track your progress each day.

Step 4: Reflect on how consistency affects your mindset.

Step 5: Extend the habit to 14 days and beyond.

Journal Prompts

1. What situations in my life currently challenge my resilience the most?
2. How do I typically respond to hardship?
3. What does “thick skin” mean to me personally?
4. When was the last time I overcame a difficult situation?
5. What lessons did I learn from past struggles?
6. How can I improve my response to pressure?
7. What external validations am I relying on too much?
8. How can I build more internal confidence?
9. What habits can I develop to strengthen my resilience?
10. What would my life look like if I fully embraced Gator Grit?

Closing Reflection

Thick skin is not about becoming unbreakable—it’s about becoming adaptable. Life will continue to present challenges, but your ability to handle them will grow. Every hardship you face is an opportunity to strengthen your resilience.

You are not defined by what happens to you. You are defined by how you respond. With Gator Grit, you learn to stand firm, adapt, and keep moving forward—no matter what comes your way.

Chapter 2: The Swamp Never Sinks: Staying Afloat in Difficult Situations

Understanding the Swamp Mindset

Life, at times, feels like a swamp—thick, heavy, slow-moving, and difficult to navigate. You don't always see what's beneath the surface, and every step can feel uncertain. The swamp represents those seasons where progress is unclear, energy is low, and everything feels like a struggle.

But here's the truth: the swamp never sinks. It may feel unstable, but it holds. It supports life, adapts to change, and continues to exist through storms, droughts, and disruption. When you adopt the swamp mindset, you begin to understand that even in the mess, there is structure.

Most people panic in the swamp because they expect solid ground. They want quick clarity, fast movement, and guaranteed outcomes. But the swamp doesn't operate that way. It requires patience, awareness, and trust in your ability to navigate without certainty.

Staying afloat in difficult situations starts with accepting the environment you're in. Resistance drains energy. Acceptance allows you to conserve it. You don't have to like the situation, but you do have to learn how to operate within it.

The swamp teaches you to move differently. Fast, aggressive action often leads to mistakes. Slow, intentional movement keeps you stable. This is not weakness—it is strategy.

There is also hidden life in the swamp. Beneath the murkiness, there are systems working, growth happening, and opportunities forming. Just because you can't see progress doesn't mean it isn't there.

This mindset shifts your perspective. Instead of feeling trapped, you begin to feel capable. You recognize that difficulty is not the end—it is a phase that requires a different approach.

The swamp does not demand perfection. It demands adaptability. When you understand that, you stop fighting the environment and start learning from it.

Stability in Unstable Conditions

Difficult situations often feel unstable because they are unfamiliar. You don't know what to expect, and that uncertainty creates anxiety. The key to staying afloat is creating internal stability when external stability is lacking.

Internal stability comes from routines, habits, and mindset. These are the anchors that keep you grounded when everything else feels unpredictable. You may not control your environment, but you can control how you respond to it.

One of the most effective ways to build stability is through consistency. Small, repeated actions create a sense of control. Even something as simple as a daily routine can provide structure in chaotic times.

Breathing, slowing down, and focusing on the present moment also play a role. When you become overwhelmed, your mind tends to jump ahead to worst-case scenarios. Grounding yourself in the present helps reduce that overwhelm.

Clarity is another form of stability. When you understand your priorities, you can navigate more effectively. You don't need to solve everything at once—you just need to focus on the next step.

It's also important to limit external noise. In difficult situations, too many opinions and distractions can increase confusion. Thick skin from the previous chapter helps here—you filter what matters and ignore what doesn't.

Stability does not mean everything is perfect. It means you are steady despite imperfection. It is the ability to remain calm, focused, and intentional even when things are uncertain.

Over time, this internal stability becomes your foundation. No matter what environment you're in, you carry that steadiness with you.

Energy Conservation and Strategic Movement

In the swamp, energy is everything. If you waste it, you sink. If you conserve it, you stay afloat. This principle applies directly to life—especially during difficult times.

Many people burn out because they try to do too much at once. They react to every problem, take on too many responsibilities, and exhaust themselves. This is the opposite of Gator Grit.

Strategic movement means choosing where to invest your energy. Not every problem needs immediate attention. Not every opportunity needs to be pursued. You must decide what truly matters.

Rest is part of this strategy. It is not laziness—it is recovery. Without rest, your ability to think clearly and act effectively decreases. Energy conservation includes knowing when to pause.

Prioritization is key. Focus on what will create the most impact. Let go of what is unnecessary. This reduces overwhelm and increases effectiveness.

It's also about pacing. You don't need to rush. Slow, steady progress is often more sustainable than bursts of intense effort followed by burnout.

Awareness plays a role here as well. Pay attention to how you spend your time and energy. Identify patterns that drain you and adjust accordingly.

When you manage your energy wisely, you become more resilient. You have the capacity to handle challenges without being depleted.

The swamp rewards those who move with intention. Every step is deliberate, every action calculated. This is how you stay afloat.

Emotional Buoyancy: Rising Above the Weight

Difficult situations often come with emotional weight—stress, fear, frustration, doubt. These emotions can pull you down if you don't know how to manage them.

Emotional buoyancy is the ability to rise above that weight. It doesn't mean ignoring your emotions—it means not letting them sink you.

The first step is awareness. You need to recognize what you're feeling without judgment. Naming your emotions reduces their intensity and gives you clarity.

Next is acceptance. Fighting your emotions often makes them stronger. Accepting them allows you to process them more effectively.

Perspective is also important. Ask yourself if the situation is as permanent or as severe as it feels in the moment. Often, emotions exaggerate reality.

Connection can help as well. Talking to someone you trust can provide relief and insight. You don't have to carry everything alone.

It's also useful to develop coping strategies—activities that help you reset emotionally. This could be journaling, walking, breathing exercises, or creative expression.

Over time, you learn to ride emotional waves instead of being overwhelmed by them. You understand that emotions are temporary.

Emotional buoyancy keeps you afloat. No matter how heavy things feel, you have the ability to rise.

Adapting Without Losing Direction

In the swamp, paths are not always clear. You may have to change direction, adjust your plans, or rethink your approach. Adaptability is essential.

However, adaptability does not mean losing your purpose. It means finding new ways to move toward it. Your destination remains the same, even if the path changes.

Flexibility allows you to respond to challenges effectively. Instead of being rigid, you become responsive. This reduces frustration and increases progress.

It's important to reassess regularly. What worked before may not work now. Being willing to adjust keeps you moving forward.

At the same time, you must stay grounded in your core values. These act as your compass. No matter how much things change, they guide your decisions.

Adaptation also involves learning. Every challenge provides information. The more you learn, the better you become at navigating future situations.

There is strength in being able to pivot without panic. It shows confidence in your ability to figure things out.

Ultimately, adaptability keeps you afloat. It allows you to move with the environment instead of being overwhelmed by it.

Trusting the Process When You Can't See the Bottom

One of the hardest parts of difficult situations is the lack of visibility. You don't always know what's ahead or how things will turn out. This uncertainty can be unsettling.

Trusting the process means continuing forward even without full clarity. It's about believing in your ability to navigate, even when you can't see the outcome.

This trust is built through experience. Every time you overcome a challenge, you reinforce the belief that you can handle the next one.

Patience is essential here. Progress is not always immediate. Sometimes, growth happens beneath the surface, unseen but significant.

It's also important to focus on what you can control. You may not control the outcome, but you can control your effort, attitude, and decisions.

Letting go of the need for certainty can be freeing. It allows you to move forward without being paralyzed by fear.

Faith in yourself plays a major role. You don't need to have all the answers—you just need to trust that you can find them.

The swamp may be unclear, but it is not endless. With persistence and trust, you will find your way through.

Alligator's Advice

The alligator does not fear the murky water. It understands that clarity is not required for survival. You don't need to see everything to move forward—you just need to trust your instincts and stay aware.

It floats with minimal effort. It does not thrash or panic. Learn to conserve your energy and let your natural buoyancy carry you when things feel heavy.

It adjusts its position constantly, even when it appears still. Small, subtle movements keep it balanced. You don't always need big changes—sometimes small adjustments are enough.

And above all, it remains calm. Panic wastes energy and clouds judgment. Stay steady, breathe, and remember—you are built to survive this.

Exercise 1: The Stability Anchor Routine

Step 1: Identify three daily habits that bring you stability (e.g., waking time, journaling, movement).

Step 2: Commit to practicing them consistently for 7 days.

Step 3: Track your consistency and note how it affects your mindset.

Step 4: Adjust and refine your habits as needed.

Step 5: Extend the routine for another 7 days to reinforce stability.

Exercise 2: Energy Audit and Reallocation

Step 1: Write down how you spent your time and energy over the past 48 hours.

Step 2: Identify activities that drained you without providing value.

Step 3: Highlight activities that supported your growth or stability.

Step 4: Reduce or eliminate one draining activity.

Step 5: Replace it with a more beneficial habit.

Exercise 3: Emotional Buoyancy Practice

Step 1: Recall a recent situation where you felt overwhelmed.

Step 2: Write down the emotions you experienced.

Step 3: Reframe the situation with a more balanced perspective.

Step 4: Identify one positive takeaway from the experience.

Step 5: Practice a calming technique (breathing, walking, journaling) when similar emotions arise.

Journal Prompts

1. What "swamp" am I currently navigating in my life?
2. How do I typically react to uncertainty?
3. What helps me feel stable during difficult times?
4. Where am I wasting energy that could be conserved?
5. How can I improve my emotional resilience?
6. What small adjustments can I make to stay afloat?
7. What does adaptability look like in my current situation?
8. How can I trust the process more fully?
9. What past experiences prove that I can overcome challenges?
10. What would it look like for me to move through this situation with Gator Grit?

Closing Reflection

The swamp is not your enemy—it is your training ground. It teaches you patience, awareness, and resilience. It forces you to slow down, conserve energy, and move with intention.

You don't need perfect conditions to stay afloat. You need stability, adaptability, and trust in yourself. The more you practice these, the stronger you become.

No matter how heavy things feel, remember this: you are not sinking—you are learning how to float.

Chapter 3: The Death Roll: Transforming Setbacks into Strength

Understanding the Death Roll Mindset

The death roll is one of the most powerful survival techniques in the natural world. When an alligator encounters resistance, it doesn't push against it in a straight line—it rotates, repositions, and uses momentum to its advantage. What seems like chaos is actually controlled transformation.

In life, setbacks are that resistance. They grip you, shake you, and threaten to pull you under. Most people respond by panicking, freezing, or trying to force their way out. But the death roll mindset teaches something different—you don't fight resistance head-on. You transform through it.

A setback is not just an obstacle. It is stored energy. It is pressure waiting to be redirected. When you learn how to "roll" with adversity instead of against it, you begin to unlock strength that wasn't available before.

This mindset requires a shift in perception. Instead of seeing failure as an endpoint, you begin to see it as raw material. Something to be shaped, refined, and repurposed. Every setback becomes something you can use.

The death roll is not about destruction—it's about control within motion. It's about staying engaged in the struggle while shifting your position until the situation no longer has power over you.

You will not avoid setbacks. They are part of the path. But you can decide how you engage with them. You can resist and exhaust yourself, or you can transform and emerge stronger.

When you adopt this mindset, you stop fearing setbacks. You start studying them. You start asking how they can serve you.

That is where real power begins—not in avoiding difficulty, but in mastering what to do when it arrives.

Breaking the Grip of Failure

Failure has a way of tightening its grip. It can make you feel stuck, defeated, and uncertain about your next move. The longer you stay in that mental space, the harder it becomes to break free.

The first step in breaking the grip of failure is separating your identity from the outcome. You are not your failure. You are someone who experienced a failure. That distinction matters more than most people realize.

When you attach your identity to failure, you internalize it. It becomes part of how you see yourself. But when you separate the two, you create space to learn and grow.

Another key step is analyzing the failure without judgment. What happened? What contributed to the outcome? What could be done differently next time? This turns failure into information.

Avoiding this analysis keeps you stuck. Facing it, even when it's uncomfortable, is what allows you to move forward.

It's also important to release the emotional weight tied to failure. Holding onto shame, regret, or frustration only prolongs the experience. Processing those emotions allows you to reset.

Support can help here. Talking through a failure with someone you trust can provide clarity and perspective. You don't have to figure everything out alone.

Breaking the grip also requires action. Even small steps forward begin to loosen the hold that failure has on you. Movement creates momentum.

Over time, failure loses its power to define you. It becomes something you navigate, not something that controls you.

Reframing Setbacks as Leverage

Every setback contains leverage. It may not feel that way in the moment, but within every challenge is something you can use to your advantage.

Reframing is the process of changing how you interpret a situation. Instead of asking, “Why did this happen to me?” you ask, “How can I use this?”

This shift opens up possibilities. What skills did you gain? What lessons did you learn? What strengths were revealed? These are all forms of leverage.

Setbacks often expose weaknesses. While uncomfortable, this is valuable information. It shows you exactly where to improve.

They also build resilience. Each time you recover from a setback, you strengthen your ability to handle future challenges.

There is also an element of clarity. Setbacks can redirect you toward better opportunities or more aligned paths. What feels like a loss can sometimes be a correction.

Leverage also comes from perspective. When you’ve experienced difficulty, you develop empathy and understanding. This can strengthen your relationships and leadership.

The key is to actively look for leverage. It doesn’t always reveal itself immediately, but it is there.

When you begin to see setbacks this way, they lose their sting. They become tools rather than threats.

Momentum Through Motion

The death roll works because of momentum. Once it begins, the motion itself creates power. In life, the same principle applies—movement generates momentum.

After a setback, the hardest part is starting again. The initial resistance is strong. Doubt, fear, and hesitation can hold you in place.

But once you take that first step, something shifts. Action creates energy. It builds confidence and reduces uncertainty.

You don't need a perfect plan to start moving. You just need a direction. Even small actions can begin the process.

Consistency amplifies this momentum. The more you move, the easier it becomes to keep moving. What once felt difficult becomes manageable.

Momentum also changes your mindset. Instead of focusing on what went wrong, you begin to focus on what you can do next.

It's important to avoid overthinking during this phase. Too much analysis can stall progress. Action provides clarity.

Over time, momentum carries you forward. The setback becomes part of your story, not the end of it.

Movement is how you regain control. It is how you turn stagnation into progress.

Emotional Alchemy: Turning Pain into Strength

Setbacks often come with emotional pain—disappointment, frustration, anger, or sadness. These emotions can either weaken you or strengthen you, depending on how you handle them.

Emotional alchemy is the process of transforming those feelings into something productive. Instead of suppressing them, you use them.

Anger can become motivation. Frustration can become focus. Sadness can deepen your understanding and empathy.

The first step is allowing yourself to feel. Ignoring emotions doesn't make them disappear—it only delays their impact.

The second step is directing them. Ask yourself how you can channel what you're feeling into action.

Creative outlets can help with this. Writing, building, creating—these activities allow you to process emotions while producing something meaningful.

Physical movement is another powerful tool. Exercise can help release tension and clear your mind.

Reflection is also important. Understanding why you feel the way you do provides insight and direction.

Over time, you learn to work with your emotions instead of against them. They become part of your strength.

Emotional alchemy turns pain into power. It transforms setbacks into fuel for growth.

Becoming Unshakeable Through Transformation

The more you engage with setbacks effectively, the more unshakeable you become. Each experience adds to your resilience.

Unshakeable does not mean unaffected. It means you can experience difficulty without losing your direction.

Transformation is the key. You are not the same person after a setback—you are someone who has learned, adapted, and grown.

This growth builds confidence. You begin to trust your ability to handle whatever comes your way.

It also creates stability. External circumstances may change, but your internal foundation remains strong.

Over time, setbacks become less intimidating. You've been through them before. You know how to respond.

This doesn't mean you seek out difficulty, but you no longer fear it. You understand that it is part of the process.

You begin to see yourself differently—not as someone who avoids hardship, but as someone who can navigate it.

That is what makes you unshakeable. Not perfection, but experience, adaptation, and growth.

Alligator's Advice

When resistance grips you, don't pull straight back. Rotate. Shift your perspective. What feels like being stuck may just be the wrong angle of approach.

Use the force against you. The struggle itself contains energy. Learn how to redirect it instead of resisting it blindly.

Stay engaged. The death roll only works because the alligator doesn't let go. Commitment is what allows transformation to happen.

And when the moment is right, finish the motion. Don't hesitate. Trust your ability to follow through and complete the transformation.

Exercise 1: Failure Reframe Practice

Step 1: Write down a recent setback or failure.

Step 2: Identify three factors that contributed to it.

Step 3: List three lessons you learned from the experience.

Step 4: Identify one way you can use those lessons moving forward.

Step 5: Take one small action based on that insight.

Exercise 2: Momentum Builder Drill

Step 1: Choose one area where you feel stuck.

Step 2: Break it down into the smallest possible action.

Step 3: Complete that action immediately.

Step 4: Repeat with another small action.

Step 5: Continue for at least 15 minutes to build momentum.

Exercise 3: Emotional Alchemy Journal

Step 1: Identify an emotion you're currently experiencing.

Step 2: Write down what triggered it.

Step 3: Explore how this emotion could be used productively.

Step 4: Create a plan to channel it into action.

Step 5: Reflect on the results after taking action.

Journal Prompts

1. What is a recent setback that impacted me deeply?
2. How did I initially respond to it?
3. What lessons can I extract from that experience?
4. How can I reframe this setback as an opportunity?
5. What small action can I take to regain momentum?
6. What emotions am I holding onto, and how can I transform them?
7. How has failure shaped my growth in the past?
8. What strengths have I developed through adversity?
9. How can I apply the death roll mindset to my current challenges?
10. What would it look like for me to become unshakeable?

Closing Reflection

Setbacks are not the end of your story—they are part of your transformation. The death roll teaches you that resistance can be used, redirected, and overcome.

You are not stuck. You are in motion, even when it doesn't feel like it. Every challenge you face is shaping you into someone stronger, more capable, and more resilient.

Trust the process. Keep moving. And remember—what tries to break you can also build you.

Chapter 4: The Power of Stillness: Learning When to Act and When to Wait

The Misunderstood Strength of Stillness

Stillness is often mistaken for inactivity, hesitation, or weakness. In a world that glorifies constant movement and nonstop action, being still can feel like falling behind. But true stillness is not the absence of action—it is controlled restraint.

Stillness is a skill. It is the ability to pause without panic, to observe without reacting, and to remain grounded while everything around you moves. This kind of control requires strength, not passivity.

Most people act too quickly because they are uncomfortable with uncertainty. They rush decisions, speak without thinking, and move without direction. This creates unnecessary problems and drains energy.

Stillness allows you to interrupt that pattern. It creates space between stimulus and response. In that space, you gain clarity.

When you practice stillness, you begin to see more. You notice patterns, details, and opportunities that would otherwise go unnoticed. Your awareness sharpens.

This awareness leads to better decisions. Instead of reacting emotionally, you respond intentionally. You act with purpose rather than impulse.

Stillness also protects your energy. You are not constantly engaging in unnecessary battles or chasing every distraction. You conserve your strength for what truly matters.

At its core, stillness is power under control. It is the foundation of strategic action.

Reading the Environment Before Moving

Before you act, you must understand where you are. Every situation has its own dynamics, and acting without awareness can lead to mistakes.

Stillness gives you the opportunity to read the environment. You observe the people, the conditions, and the patterns at play. This information becomes your advantage.

Most people skip this step. They move based on assumptions rather than observation. This often leads to missteps and setbacks.

When you slow down, you gather data. You notice what is stable and what is shifting. You identify potential risks and opportunities.

This process is not about overthinking—it is about informed awareness. You are preparing yourself to act effectively when the time comes.

Timing is influenced by your understanding of the environment. Acting too early or too late can change the outcome significantly.

Stillness allows you to align your actions with the right moment. You are not guessing—you are responding to what is actually happening.

Over time, this skill becomes intuitive. You develop a sense of when to move and when to wait.

Reading the environment is what turns stillness into strategy.

Resisting the Urge to React

One of the biggest challenges in developing stillness is resisting the urge to react. Emotions, pressure, and external stimuli can push you toward immediate action.

Reaction is often driven by fear, frustration, or impatience. It feels urgent, but it is rarely effective.

Stillness gives you the ability to pause. Instead of reacting instantly, you take a moment to assess the situation.

This pause changes everything. It allows you to choose your response rather than being controlled by your emotions.

It also prevents unnecessary escalation. Many conflicts and problems arise from reactive behavior. Stillness helps you avoid these situations.

Developing this skill requires practice. You must train yourself to recognize when you are about to react and consciously choose to pause.

Breathing techniques, mental cues, and awareness can help with this. The goal is to create a habit of intentional response.

Over time, you become less reactive and more controlled. Your actions are deliberate rather than impulsive.

This control is a key component of resilience. It keeps you steady in unpredictable situations.

Patience as a Strategic Advantage

Patience is often seen as waiting passively, but in reality, it is an active skill. It requires discipline, focus, and trust in the process.

When you are patient, you give situations time to develop. You allow opportunities to reveal themselves and problems to resolve naturally.

Impatience, on the other hand, leads to rushed decisions and missed opportunities. It creates unnecessary stress and reduces effectiveness.

Patience works hand in hand with stillness. While stillness keeps you grounded, patience keeps you committed to the right timing.

This combination allows you to act with precision. You are not forced into action—you choose it.

Patience also builds resilience. It teaches you to endure uncertainty without losing focus.

It's important to understand that patience is not about doing nothing. It's about doing the right thing at the right time.

This requires trust—trust in yourself, in your preparation, and in the process.

When you develop patience, you gain a significant advantage. You are no longer controlled by urgency.

Knowing When to Strike

Stillness is not permanent. It is a phase that prepares you for action. When the moment is right, you must be ready to move.

Knowing when to act is just as important as knowing when to wait. This is where observation, patience, and awareness come together.

The right moment often presents itself through clarity. You see the opportunity, understand the risks, and feel aligned with the decision.

Hesitation at this stage can cause you to miss the moment. Once you decide to act, you must commit fully.

This is where confidence comes in. Trusting your preparation allows you to move without doubt.

Action should be precise and intentional. You are not reacting—you are executing.

It's also important to accept that not every action will be perfect. The goal is not perfection, but progress.

Each action provides feedback. You learn, adjust, and continue moving forward.

Knowing when to strike is the result of mastering stillness.

Balancing Action and Stillness

The ultimate goal is balance. Too much stillness can lead to stagnation, while too much action can lead to burnout.

You need both. Stillness provides clarity and control. Action creates progress and results.

The key is knowing when to shift between the two. This requires awareness and adaptability.

When you feel overwhelmed, stillness can help you reset. When you feel stuck, action can help you move forward.

This balance creates a rhythm. You observe, wait, act, and adjust. This cycle becomes your approach to life.

Over time, this rhythm becomes natural. You no longer have to think about it—it becomes part of how you operate.

This balance also reduces stress. You are not constantly forcing action or resisting stillness.

Instead, you move with intention. You align your actions with the situation.

This is the essence of Gator Grit—controlled strength, strategic movement, and steady resilience.

Alligator's Advice

The alligator can remain still for hours, watching, waiting, conserving energy. It does not rush. Learn to be comfortable in stillness—it is where clarity is formed.

It studies its environment before moving. Every detail matters. Pay attention to what is happening around you before you act.

When it moves, it moves with purpose. No wasted motion, no hesitation. When your moment comes, commit fully.

And if the moment is not right, it waits. There is no panic in waiting—only preparation. Trust that the right time will come.

Exercise 1: The Stillness Practice

Step 1: Set aside 10 minutes each day for quiet reflection.

Step 2: Sit in a comfortable position and focus on your breathing.

Step 3: Observe your thoughts without reacting to them.

Step 4: Bring your focus back to your breath when your mind wanders.

Step 5: Reflect on how this practice affects your awareness and decision-making.

Exercise 2: Reaction Control Drill

Step 1: Identify a situation where you tend to react quickly.

Step 2: The next time it occurs, pause for 5 seconds before responding.

Step 3: Use that time to assess your emotions and the situation.

Step 4: Choose a response that aligns with your goals.

Step 5: Reflect on the outcome and adjust your approach.

Exercise 3: Timing Awareness Exercise

Step 1: Think of a decision you need to make.

Step 2: Write down the pros and cons of acting now versus waiting.

Step 3: Observe the situation for 24 hours without taking action.

Step 4: Reassess with new information.

Step 5: Make a decision based on clarity rather than urgency.

4

Journal Prompts

1. How do I currently respond to uncertainty?
2. When was the last time I acted too quickly?
3. What did I learn from that experience?
4. How can I improve my ability to stay still?
5. What situations require more patience from me?
6. How do I know when it's time to act?
7. What triggers my reactive behavior?
8. How can I develop better control over my responses?
9. What does balance between action and stillness look like for me?
10. How can I apply stillness to my current challenges?

Closing Reflection

Stillness is not a pause in progress—it is part of it. It is where clarity is built, where strategy is formed, and where strength is conserved.

When you learn to embrace stillness, you gain control over your actions. You stop reacting and start responding with intention.

And when the time comes to act, you do so with precision, confidence, and purpose.

Chapter 5: Survival Mode: How to Keep Going When Things Get Rough

What Survival Mode Really Means

Survival mode is often misunderstood as something negative—a state of stress, urgency, and constant pressure. And while it can feel that way, survival mode is also one of the most powerful human functions. It is your built-in system for enduring when conditions are not ideal.

At its core, survival mode is about continuation. It is not about thriving, excelling, or optimizing—it is about keeping yourself moving forward when everything feels like it's falling apart.

There are seasons in life where growth slows, clarity fades, and energy drops. These are not failure seasons. These are survival seasons. Recognizing the difference is critical.

When you mislabel survival as failure, you become discouraged. You think you're falling behind when, in reality, you're holding your ground. Survival mode reframes that—it shows you that staying afloat is progress.

This mode simplifies your priorities. You are no longer focused on everything—you are focused on what matters most. What keeps you stable? What keeps you going?

It also strips away unnecessary pressure. You don't need to be perfect. You don't need to do everything. You just need to continue.

Survival mode is not where you stay forever, but it is where you build endurance. It strengthens your ability to handle difficult conditions.

Understanding survival mode removes guilt. It allows you to operate with clarity instead of self-judgment.

Reducing Life to Essential Functions

When things get rough, complexity becomes your enemy. The more overwhelmed you are, the more important it is to simplify.

Survival mode is about reducing life to its essential functions. What do you need to maintain stability? Food, rest, basic responsibilities, and mental clarity.

This is not the time for overextension. It is the time for focus. You identify what is necessary and let go of what is not.

Many people struggle here because they try to maintain their normal pace during difficult times. This leads to burnout and deeper stress.

Simplification is not giving up—it is strategic adjustment. You are conserving your resources so you can endure.

It's important to create a minimal structure. A simple routine can provide stability even when everything else feels uncertain.

You also need to protect your energy. This means saying no to unnecessary commitments and limiting distractions.

Reducing your focus allows you to perform better in the areas that matter. It keeps you from being spread too thin.

Survival mode teaches you that less can be more—especially when things are tough.

Mental Endurance in Difficult Times

Your mind plays a critical role in survival. When things get rough, your thoughts can either support you or work against you.

Negative thinking can amplify stress and make situations feel worse than they are. It creates a loop of doubt, fear, and frustration.

Mental endurance is about breaking that loop. It's about choosing thoughts that support your ability to continue.

This doesn't mean ignoring reality. It means interpreting it in a way that keeps you functional.

Self-talk is a powerful tool. What you say to yourself matters. Encouraging, realistic thoughts can help you stay grounded.

It's also important to manage information. Too much negative input—news, opinions, distractions—can overwhelm your mind.

Focus on what you can control. This reduces anxiety and gives you a sense of direction.

Mental endurance is built through repetition. The more you practice supportive thinking, the stronger it becomes.

Over time, your mind becomes an ally rather than an obstacle.

Physical and Emotional Preservation

Survival mode requires you to take care of your physical and emotional state. You cannot endure if you are completely depleted.

Sleep, nutrition, and movement become essential. They are not optional—they are foundational.

Even small actions can make a difference. Drinking water, taking a short walk, or resting when needed can help maintain your energy.

Emotionally, you need to create space for yourself. You cannot carry everything at once.

This might mean setting boundaries, limiting interactions, or taking time to process your feelings.

It's also important to avoid self-neglect. When things get hard, it's easy to stop taking care of yourself. This only makes the situation worse.

Preservation is not weakness—it is strategy. You are maintaining your capacity to continue.

Over time, these small acts of care add up. They keep you stable and prevent burnout.

Your ability to survive depends on how well you preserve yourself.

Adapting Expectations Without Losing Hope

In survival mode, expectations need to change. What was possible before may not be possible now.

Holding yourself to the same standards can create unnecessary pressure. It can make you feel like you're failing when you're actually adapting.

Adjusting expectations allows you to be realistic. It helps you focus on what you can do rather than what you can't.

This doesn't mean lowering your goals permanently. It means recognizing that you are in a different phase.

Hope is still important. You are not giving up on your future—you are navigating your present.

Balancing realism and hope is key. You acknowledge the difficulty while still believing in improvement.

This mindset keeps you moving forward. It prevents you from becoming stuck in negativity.

Adaptation is a sign of strength. It shows that you are responding to your environment rather than being controlled by it.

Over time, as conditions improve, you can expand your expectations again.

The Power of Persistence

Survival mode is sustained by persistence. It is the decision to keep going, even when it's hard.

Persistence is not about intensity—it is about consistency. Small, repeated actions create progress.

There will be days when you don't feel motivated. That's normal. Persistence means continuing anyway.

It's important to focus on the next step, not the entire journey. Breaking things down makes them more manageable.

Each step forward builds momentum. Even slow progress is still progress.

Persistence also builds confidence. The more you continue, the more you trust your ability to endure.

It's not about how fast you move—it's about not stopping.

Over time, persistence turns survival into recovery, and recovery into growth.

This is how you move through difficult times—one step at a time.

Alligator's Advice

When the environment becomes harsh, the alligator does not panic—it conserves. You don't need to do everything right now. Focus on what keeps you going.

It slows its movements to preserve energy. You don't have to move fast—just don't stop completely.

It adapts to the conditions around it. If the situation changes, adjust. Survival depends on flexibility.

And above all, it endures. It stays in the environment as long as necessary. You are built to last longer than the storm.

Exercise 1: Essential Focus Reset

Step 1: Write down everything currently on your plate.

Step 2: Identify the top three essentials that must be maintained.

Step 3: Temporarily eliminate or reduce non-essential tasks.

Step 4: Create a simple daily plan around your essentials.

Step 5: Review and adjust as needed.

Exercise 2: Mental Endurance Practice

Step 1: Identify a recurring negative thought.

Step 2: Write it down.

Step 3: Challenge it with a more balanced perspective.

Step 4: Repeat the new thought daily.

Step 5: Observe how it affects your mindset over time.

Exercise 3: Energy Preservation Routine

Step 1: Identify one habit that drains your energy.

Step 2: Reduce or eliminate it for 7 days.

Step 3: Replace it with a restorative activity (rest, movement, hydration).

Step 4: Track how you feel each day.

Step 5: Continue or adjust based on results.

Journal Prompts

1. What does survival mode look like in my life right now?
2. What are my current essential priorities?
3. How can I simplify my daily routine?
4. What thoughts are helping or hurting my ability to continue?
5. How can I better preserve my energy?
6. What expectations do I need to adjust?
7. What does persistence mean to me?
8. How have I survived difficult times in the past?
9. What small steps can I take today?
10. How can I maintain hope during this phase?

Closing Reflection

Survival mode is not a setback—it is a phase of endurance. It is where you learn to keep going, even when things are difficult.

You don't need to be perfect. You don't need to have everything figured out. You just need to continue.

And as long as you keep moving, you are not losing—you are surviving.

Appendix A: Daily Resilience Practices Inspired by Alligators

Resilience is not built in rare, dramatic moments—it is built daily, through small, repeatable actions that strengthen your mind, body, and awareness. The alligator does not rely on luck or bursts of effort to survive. It relies on consistency, efficiency, and instinct sharpened over time. This appendix translates those principles into practical daily practices you can use to develop unshakable resilience.

Practice 1: The Still Water Morning Ritual (Awareness & Grounding)

This practice is designed to help you begin your day with clarity, control, and calm focus. Just as an alligator rests just beneath the surface, alert but still, you will train your mind to be steady and aware before the day's demands begin.

Step 1: Wake up and sit in a quiet space before engaging with your phone, conversations, or external distractions. This is your controlled environment.

Step 2: Close your eyes and take slow, deep breaths. Inhale through your nose for 4 seconds, hold for 2 seconds, and exhale through your mouth for 6 seconds. Repeat this cycle for at least 3–5 minutes.

Step 3: As you breathe, observe your thoughts without reacting to them. Let them pass like movement on the surface of water. Do not chase or suppress them—just notice.

Step 4: Bring your awareness to your body. Notice tension, tightness, or discomfort. Relax those areas consciously, starting from your head and moving down to your feet.

Step 5: Set a clear intention for the day. Not a long list—just one focus. It could be staying calm under pressure, completing a task, or conserving your energy.

Step 6: Visualize yourself moving through the day with control and steadiness. Imagine challenges arising and you responding with patience and clarity.

Step 7: Open your eyes slowly and begin your day without rushing. Carry that stillness with you into your first action.

Step 8: Avoid immediate chaos. Delay checking messages or engaging with stress triggers for at least 10–15 minutes after this practice.

This ritual builds awareness, emotional control, and intentional action. Over time, it trains you to start each day from a place of strength instead of reaction.

Practice 2: The Energy Conservation Cycle (Efficiency & Endurance)

This practice helps you manage your energy throughout the day so you don't burn out. Like an alligator that moves only when necessary, you will learn to conserve energy and act with purpose.

Step 1: At the start of your work period, identify your top three essential tasks. These should be the actions that create the most impact—not the most noise.

Step 2: Break each task into smaller steps. This reduces overwhelm and makes it easier to maintain focus.

Step 3: Work in focused intervals (for example, 25–45 minutes). During this time, eliminate distractions—no multitasking, no unnecessary interruptions.

Step 4: After each interval, take a short recovery break (5–10 minutes). Step away, stretch, hydrate, or rest your eyes. This is your energy reset.

Step 5: During breaks, avoid draining activities like scrolling or overthinking. Keep your recovery intentional.

Step 6: Pay attention to your energy levels. Notice when you feel focused versus when you feel fatigued. Adjust your workload accordingly.

Step 7: If you feel overwhelmed, pause instead of pushing through blindly. Reset, then continue with a clear mind.

Step 8: At the end of the day, review how you spent your energy. Identify what worked and what drained you unnecessarily.

This cycle teaches you how to work smarter, not harder. It builds endurance by preventing burnout and keeping your energy aligned with your priorities.

Practice 3: The Adaptation Reflection Drill (Growth & Transformation)

This practice is designed to help you turn daily challenges into long-term strength. Like an alligator adapting to its environment, you will learn to adjust, reflect, and improve continuously.

Step 1: At the end of your day, set aside 10–15 minutes for reflection. Choose a quiet space where you can think clearly.

Step 2: Identify one challenge or difficult moment you experienced during the day. It can be small or significant.

Step 3: Write down what happened without exaggeration or judgment. Focus on facts, not emotions.

Step 4: Analyze your response. How did you react? What worked? What didn't?

Step 5: Identify one lesson from the experience. What did this situation teach you about yourself or your approach?

Step 6: Decide how you would handle a similar situation in the future. Create a simple plan or adjustment.

Step 7: Acknowledge what you did well. Even in difficult situations, there is always something you handled correctly.

Step 8: Close the reflection with a reset mindset. Leave the situation in the past and prepare to apply your insight moving forward.

This drill builds self-awareness, adaptability, and continuous improvement. It turns daily experiences into long-term resilience.

Closing Reflection

Resilience is not built in isolation—it is built through daily practice. The stillness you create in the morning, the energy you manage throughout the day, and the reflections you make at night all contribute to your strength.

The alligator does not survive because it is the fastest or the most aggressive. It survives because it is efficient, aware, and adaptable. It knows when to move, when to wait, and how to conserve its energy for what matters most.

These practices are your foundation. They may seem simple, but their power comes from consistency. When you repeat them daily, they begin to shape how you think, act, and respond to life.

Over time, resilience stops being something you try to build—it becomes part of who you are.

You don't need to rush the process.

You just need to stay consistent.

Message from the Author:

I hope you enjoyed this book, I love astrology and knew there was not a book such as this out on the shelf. I love metaphysical items as well. Please check out my other books:

-Life of Government Benefits

-My life of Hell

-My life with Hydrocephalus

-Red Sky

-World Domination:Woman's rule

-World Domination:Woman's Rule 2: The War

-Life and Banishment of Apophis: book 1

-The Kidney Friendly Diet

-The Ultimate Hemp Cookbook

-Creating a Dispensary(legally)

-Cleanliness throughout life: the importance of showering from childhood to adulthood.

-Strong Roots: The Risks of Overcoddling children

-Hemp Horoscopes: Cosmic Insights and Earthly Healing

- Celestial Hemp Navigating the Zodiac: Through the Green Cosmos

-Astrological Hemp: Aligning The Stars with Earth's Ancient Herb

-The Astrological Guide to Hemp: Stars, Signs, and Sacred Leaves

-Green Growth: Innovative Marketing Strategies for your Hemp Products and Dispensary

-Cosmic Cannabis

-Astrological Munchies

-Henry The Hemp

-Zodiacal Roots: The Astrological Soul Of Hemp

- **Green Constellations: Intersection of Hemp and Zodiac**

-Hemp in The Houses: An astrological Adventure Through The Cannabis Galaxy

-Galactic Ganja Guide

Heavenly Hemp

Zodiac Leaves

Doctor Who Astrology

Cannastrology

Stellar Satvias and Cosmic Indicas

Celestial Cannabis: A Zodiac Journey

AstroHerbology: The Sky and The Soil: Volume 1

AstroHerbology:Celestial Cannabis:Volume 2

Cosmic Cannabis Cultivation

The Starry Guide to Herbal Harmony: Volume 1

The Starry Guide to Herbal Harmony: Cannabis Universe: Volume 2

Yugioh Astrology: Astrological Guide to Deck, Duels and more

Nightmare Mansion: Echoes of The Abyss

Nightmare Mansion 2: Legacy of Shadows

Nightmare Mansion 3: Shadows of the Forgotten

Nightmare Mansion 4: Echoes of the Damned

The Life and Banishment of Apophis: Book 2

Nightmare Mansion: Halls of Despair

Healing with Herb: Cannabis and Hydrocephalus

Planetary Pot: Aligning with Astrological Herbs: Volume 1

Fast Track to Freedom: 30 Days to Financial Independence Using AI, Assets, and Agile Hustles

Cosmic Hemp Pathways

How to Become Financially Free in 30 Days: 10,000 Paths to Prosperity

Zodiacal Herbage: Astrological Insights: Volume 1

Nightmare Mansion: Whispers in the Walls

The Daleks Invade Atlantis

Henry the hemp and Hydrocephalus

10X The Kidney Friendly Diet

Cannabis Universe: Adult coloring book

Hemp Astrology: The Healing Power of the Stars

Zodiacal Herbage: Astrological Insights: Cannabis Universe: Volume 2

Planetary Pot: Aligning with Astrological Herbs: Cannabis Universes: Volume 2

Doctor Who: Convergence Protocol – The Replicator War

Nightmare Mansion: Curse of the Blood Moon

The Celestial Stoner: A Guide to the Zodiac

Cosmic Pleasures: Sex Toy Astrology for Every Sign

Hydrocephalus Astrology: Navigating the Stars and Healing Waters

Lapis and the Mischievous Chocolate Bar

Celestial Positions: Sexual Astrology for Every Sign

Apophis's Shadow Work Journal: **:** A Journey of Self-Discovery and Healing

Kinky Cosmos: Sexual Kink Astrology for Every Sign

Digital Cosmos: The Astrological Digimon Compendium

Stellar Seeds: The Cosmic Guide to Growing with Astrology

Apophis's Daily Gratitude Journal

Cat Astrology: Feline Mysteries of the Cosmos

The Cosmic Kama Sutra: An Astrological Guide to Sexual Positions

Unleash Your Potential: A Guided Journal Powered by AI Insights

Whispers of the Enchanted Grove

Cosmic Pleasures: An Astrological Guide to Sexual Kinks

369, 12 Manifestation Journal

Whisper of the nocturne journal(blank journal for writing or drawing)

The Boogey Book

Locked In Reflection: A Chastity Journey Through Locktober

Generating Wealth Quickly:How to Generate $100,000 in 24 Hours

Star Magic: Harness the Power of the Universe

The Flatulence Chronicles: A Fart Journal for Self-Discovery

The Doctor and The Death Moth

Seize the Day: A Personal Seizure Tracking Journal

The Ultimate Boogeyman Safari: A Journey into the Boogie World and Beyond

Whispers of Samhain: 1,000 Spells of Love, Luck, and Lunar Magic: Samhain Spell Book

Apophis's guides:Witch's Spellbook Crafting Guide for Halloween

Frost & Flame: The Enchanted Yule Grimoire of 1000 Winter Spells

The Ultimate Boogey Goo Guide & Spooky Activities for Halloween Fun

Harmony of the Scales: A Libra's Spellcraft for Balance and Beauty

The Enchanted Advent: 36 Days of Christmas Wonders

Nightmare Mansion: The Labyrinth of Screams

Harvest of Enchantment: 1,000 Spells of Gratitude, Love, and Fortune for Thanksgiving

The Boogey Chronicles: A Journal of Nightly Encounters and Shadowy Secrets

The 12 Days of Financial Freedom: A Step-by-Step Christmas Countdown to Transform Your Finances

Sigil of the Eternal Spiral Blank Journal

A Christmas Feast: Timeless Recipes for Every Meal

Holiday Stress-Free Solutions: A Survival Guide to Thriving During the Festive Season

Yu-Gi-Oh! Holiday Gifting Mastery: The Ultimate Guide for Fans and Newcomers Alike

Holiday Harmony: A Hydrocephalus Survival Guide for the Festive Season

Celestial Craft: The Witch's Almanac for 2025 – A Cosmic Guide to Manifestations, Moons, and Mystical Events

Doctor Who: The Toymaker's Winter Wonderland

Tulsa King Unveiled: A Thrilling Guide to Stallone's Mafia Masterpiece

Pendulum Craft: A Complete Guide to Crafting and Using Personalized Divination Tools

Nightmare Mansion: Santa's Eternal Eve

Starlight Noel: A Cosmic Journey through Christmas Mysteries

The Dark Architect: Unlocking the Blueprint of Existence

Surviving the Embrace: The Ultimate Guide to Encounters with The Hugging Molly

The Enchanted Codex: Secrets of the Craft for Witches, Wiccans, and Pagans

Harvest of Gratitude: A Complete Thanksgiving Guide

Yuletide Essentials: A Complete Guide to an Authentic and Magical Christmas

Celestial Smokes: A Cosmic Guide to Cigars and Astrology

Living in Balance: A Comprehensive Survival Guide to Thriving with Diabetes Insipidus

Cosmic Symbiosis: The Venom Zodiac Chronicles

The Cursed Paw of Ambition

Cosmic Symbiosis: The Astrological Venom Journal

Celestial Wonders Unfold: A Stargazer's Guide to the Cosmos (2024-2029)

The Ultimate Black Friday Prepper's Guide: Mastering Shopping Strategies and Savings

Cosmic Sales: The Astrological Guide to Black Friday Shopping

Legends of the Corn Mother and Other Harvest Myths

Whispers of the Harvest: The Corn Mother's Journal

The Evergreen Spellbook

The Doctor Meets the Boogeyman

The White Witch of Rose Hall's SpellBook

The Gingerbread Golem's Shadow: A Study in Sweet Darkness

The Gingerbread Golem Codex: An Academic Exploration of Sweet Myths

The Gingerbread Golem Grimoire: Sweet Magicks and Spells for the Festive Witch

The Curse of the Gingerbread Golem

10-minute Christmas Crafts for kids

Christmas Crisis Solutions: The Ultimate Last-Minute Survival Guide

Gingerbread Golem Recipes: Holiday Treats with a Magical Twist

The Infinite Key: Unlocking Mystical Secrets of the Ages

Enchanted Yule: A Wiccan and Pagan Guide to a Magical and Memorable Season

Dinosaurs of Power: Unlocking Ancient Magick

Astro-Dinos: The Cosmic Guide to Prehistoric Wisdom

Gallifrey's Yule Logs: A Festive Doctor Who Cookbook

The Dino Grimoire: Secrets of Prehistoric Magick

The Gift They Never Knew They Needed

The Gingerbread Golem's Culinary Alchemy: Enchanting Recipes for a Sweetly Dark Feast

A Time Lord Christmas: Holiday Adventures with the Doctor

Krampusproofing Your Home: Defensive Strategies for Yule

Silent Frights: A Collection of Christmas Creepypastas to Chill Your Bones

Santa Raptor's Jolly Carnage: A Dino-Claus Christmas Tale

Prehistoric Palettes: A Dino Wicca Coloring Journey

The Christmas Wishkeeper Chronicles

The Starlight Sleigh: A Holiday Journey

Elf Secrets: The True Magic of the North Pole

Candy Cane Conjurations

Cooking with Kids: Recipes Under 20 Minutes

Doctor Who: The TARDIS Confiscation

The Anxiety First Aid Kit: Quick Tools to Calm Your Mind

Frosty Whispers: A Winter's Tale

The Infinite Key: Unlocking the Secrets to Prosperity, Resilience, and Purpose

The Grasping Void: Why You'll Regret This Purchase

Astrology for Busy Bees: Star Signs Simplified

The Instant Focus Formula: Cut Through the Noise

The Secret Language of Colors: Unlocking the Emotional Codes

Sacred Fossil Chronicles: Blank Journal

The Christmas Cottage Miracle

Feeding Frenzy: Graboid-Inspired Recipes

Manifest in Minutes: The Quick Law of Attraction Guide

The Symbiote Chronicles: Doctor Who's Venomous Journey

Think Tiny, Grow Big: The Minimalist Mindset

The Energy Key: Unlocking Limitless Motivation

New Year, New Magic: Manifesting Your Best Year Yet

Unstoppable You: Mastering Confidence in Minutes

Infinite Energy: The Secret to Never Feeling Drained

Lightning Focus: Mastering the Art of Productivity in a Distracted World

Saturnalia Manifestation Magick: A Guide to Unlocking Abundance During the Solstice

Graboids and Garland: The Ultimate Tremors-Themed Christmas Guide

12 Nights of Holiday Magic

The Power of Pause: 60-Second Mindfulness Practices

The Quick Reset: How to Reclaim Your Life After Burnout

The Shadow Eater: A Tale of Despair and Survival

The Micro-Mastery Method: Transform Your Skills in Just Minutes a Day

Reclaiming Time: How to Live More by Doing Less
Chronovore: The Eternal Nexus
The Mind Reset: Unlocking Your Inner Peace in a Chaotic World
Confidence Code: Building Unshakable Self-Belief
Baby the Vampire Terrier
Baby the Vampire Terrier's Christmas Adventure
Celestial Streams: The Content Creator's Astrology Manual
The Wealth Whisperer: Unlocking Abundance with Everyday Actions
The Energy Equation: Maximize Your Output Without Burning Out
The Happiness Algorithm: Science-Backed Steps to Joyful Living
Stress-Free Success: Achieving Goals Without Anxiety
Mindful Wealth: The New Blueprint for Financial Freedom
The Festive Flavors of New Year: A Culinary Celebration
The Master's Gambit: Keys of Eternal Power
Shadowed Secrets: Groundhog Day Mysteries
Beneath the Burrow: Lessons from the Groundhog
Spring's Whispers: The Groundhog's Prediction
The Limitless Mindset: Unlock Your Untapped Potential
The Focus Funnel: How to Cut Through Chaos and Get Results
Bold Moves: Building Courage to Live on Your Terms
The Daily Shift: Simple Practices for Lasting Transformation
The Quarter-Life Reset: Thriving in Your 20s and 30s
The Art of Shadowplay: Building Your Own Personal Myth
The Eternal Loop: Finding Purpose in Repetition
Burrowing Wisdom: Life Lessons from the Groundhog
Shadow Work: A Groundhog Day Perspective
Love in Bloom: 5-Minute Romantic Gestures
The Shadowspell Codex: Secrets of Forbidden Magick
The Burnout Cure: Finding Balance in a Busy World
The Groundhog Prophecy: Unlocking Seasonal Secrets
Nog Tales: The Spirited History of Eggnog

Six More Weeks: Embracing Seasonal Transitions
The Lumivian Chronicles: Fragments of the Fifth Dimension
Money on Your Mind: A Beginner's Guide to Wealth
The Focus Fix: Breaking Through Distraction
January's Spirit Keepers: Mystical Protectors of the Cold
Creativity Unchained: Unlocking Your Wildest Ideas in 2025
Manifestation Mastery: 365 Days to Rewrite Your Reality
The Groundhog's Mirror: Reflecting on Change
The Weeping Angels' Christmas Curse
Burrowed in Time: A Groundhog Day Journey
Heartbeats: Poems to Share with Your Valentine
Dino Wicca: The Sacred Grimoire of Prehistoric Magick
Courage of the Pride: Finding Your Inner Roar
The Lion's Leap: Bold Moves for Big Results
Healthy Hustle: Achieving Without Overworking
Practical Manifesting: Turning Dreams into Reality in 2025
Jurassic Pharaohs: Unlocking the Magick of Ancient Egypt and Dino Wicca
The Happiness Equation: Small Changes for Big Joy
The Confidence Compass: Finding Your Inner Strength
Whispers in the Hollow: Tales of the Forgotten Beasts
Echoes from the Hollow: The Return of Forgotten Beasts
The Hollow Ascendant: The Rise of the Forgotten Beasts
The Relationship Reset: Building Better Connections
Mastering the Morning: How to Win the Day Before 8 AM
The Shadow's Dance: Groundhog Day Symbolism
Cupid's Kitchen: Quick Valentine's Day Recipes
Valentine's Day on a Budget: Love Without Breaking the Bank
Astrocraft: Aligning the Stars in the World of Minecraft
Forecasting Life: Groundhog Day Reflections
Bleeding Hearts: Twisted Tales of Valentine's Terror
Herbal Smoke Revolution: The Ultimate Guide to Nature's Cigarette Alternative

Winter's Wrath: The Complete Survival Blueprint for Extreme Freezes.

The Groundhog's Shadow: A Tale of Seasons

Burrowed Insights: Wisdom from the Groundhog

Sensual Strings: The Art of Erotic Bondage

Whispered Flames: Unlocking the Power of Fire Play

Forgotten Shadows: A Guide to Cryptids Lost to Time

Six Weeks of Secrets: Groundhog Day's Hidden Messages

Shadows and Cycles: Groundhog Day Reflections

The Art of Love Letters: Crafting the Perfect Message

Romantic Getaways at Home: Turning Your Space into Paradise

Purrfect Brews: A Cat Lover's Guide to Coffee and Companionship

The Groundhog's Wisdom: Timeless Lessons for Modern Life

The Shadow Oracle: Groundhog Day as a Predictor

Emerging from the Burrow: A Journey of Renewal

The Language of Love: Learning Your Partner's Love Style

Authorpreneur: The Ultimate Blueprint for Writing, Publishing, and Thriving as an Author

Weathering the Seasons: Groundhog Day Perspectives

Valentine's Day Magic: A Guide to Romantic Rituals

The Shadow Chronicles: Stories of Groundhog Day

Love and Laughter: Fun Games for Valentine's Day

AstroRealty: Unlocking the Stars for Property Success

The Groundhog's Path: A Guide to Seasonal Balance

Groundhog Day Diaries: Reflections in the Shadow

The Groundhog's Light: Illuminating the Path Ahead

Valentine's Traditions from Around the World

AI Wealth Revolution: Unlocking the Trillionaire Mindset

Love Rekindled: Reigniting Passion in Relationships

Single and Thriving: Self-Love on Valentine's Day

Emerald Legends: Mystical Tales of Ireland

Green Alchemy: Harnessing Nature's Magic
The Hearts of Horror: A Valentine's Day Nightmare
The Leprechaun's Guide to Wealth and Wisdom
Dancing with the Sidhe: Celebrating the Otherworld
Shamrocks and Shadows: Mysteries of the Green Isle
Emerald Energy: Harnessing Luck and Growth
The Gingerbread Golem's Valentine: A Sweetheart's Guide to Love and Enchantment
The Celtic Knot: Weaving Life and Destiny
Green Fire: Elemental Magic for St. Patrick's Day
Clover Chronicles: Finding Your Inner Luck
Ireland's Mystical Creatures: A Field Guide
Gingerbread Golem's Love Almanac
Prowl and Thrive: The Lion's Guide to Success
Love Alchemy: Transforming Your Life Through Heart Energy
WORLD DOMINATION: Woman's Rule 3:The New Life
The Midnight Rose: A Guide to Lunar Love Spells
The Forbidden Letters: Writing Your Own Love Prophecy
Luck and Lore: St. Patrick's Day for Modern Mystics
The Green Path: A Pagan Celebration of Renewal
The Dark Architect's Guide to Reprogramming Reality
Prankster's Paradise: A Guide to Harmless Hijinks
Manifest Your Reality: The Law of Attraction Simplified
The TARDIS Owner's Manual: Understanding the Doctor's Ship: *A complete guide to the TARDIS, its technology, secrets, and mysteries*
Starlit Romance: Astrology Secrets for Finding True Love
The Time Lord's Atlas: A Complete Guide to the Whoniverse: ***A breakdown of the locations, planets, and dimensions explored in Doctor Who***
Sweetheart Shadows: The Dark Side of Love and Attraction
February Fire: Reigniting Passion in Every Area of Life

The Self-Love Toolkit: 5 Ways to Embrace Who You Are

February Sparks: Ignite Your Dreams in 28 Days

March to Success: A 31-Day Action Blueprint

Ancient Paths: The 13 Sacred Principles of Dino Wicca

Echoes of Tomorrow: Navigating the AI Revolution

The Wellness Blueprint: Balancing Mind, Body, and Soul

Green Horizons: Sustainable Living for a Better Tomorrow

The AI Wealth Code: How to Make Millions with Automation

AI-Powered Creativity: Writing, Art, and Music for Profit

Extinction Rites: Rebirthing Your Soul Through Prehistoric Magick

Sacred Serpents tarot

Celestial Enchantment blank journal

Star Strains

Culinary Journeys: Exploring Global Flavors at Home

The Hollowvale Curse

The Hollowvale Harvest

The Egg of Transformation: Awakening Your Inner Power

Blooming Into Power: A Wiccan Guide to Spring Awakening

The Nightmare Nexus: The Third Doctor's Perilous Haunting

Digital Detox: Reclaiming Your Life in a Connected World

Ostara's Path: Walking the Spiral of Renewal

The Sacred Hare

Financial Freedom: Building Wealth in the Modern Age

Spring's Cauldron: Stirring the Waters of Change

The Hollowvale Pact

Quantum Consciousness: The Science of Reality Shifting

The Hollowvale Hunger

The Sacred Waters Within: A Witch's Guide to Hydrocephalus Magick

The Raven's Nest: Building a Life of Unshakable Stability

AI and the Human Mind: The Future of Intelligence

The Hollowvale Reckoning

Timeless Love: Building and Maintaining Lasting Relationships

The Raven's Roar: Unlocking Unstoppable Confidence

Raven Sight: Awakening Intuition and Inner Wisdom

The Butterfly Effect: Small Changes, Big Transformations

Taming the Boogeyman: How to Conquer Your Inner Fears

The Magick of Green: Awakening Earth's Energy in You

The Entrepreneurial Mindset: Secrets to Business Success

The Hollowvale End

The Shadow Luck Ritual: Reclaiming Power from Your Dark Side

Spring Magick for Beginners: A Simple Guide to Seasonal Energy Work

Doctor Who: The Hollowvale Conundrum

The March of Miracles: Unlocking Synchronicities in Spring

Unveiling the Cosmos: A Guide to Stargazing and Space Exploration

The Ultimate Guide to Surviving an Economic Collapse

The AI Gold Rush: How to Profit from the AI Revolution

Bastet's Shadow: The Hidden Power of Feline Magick

The Bastet Codex: Unlocking the Goddess's Magickal Secrets

Purring Spells: Harnessing Bastet's Healing Frequencies

Bastet's Nine Lives: Rebirth, Transformation, and Immortality Spells

Primal Currents: Hydrocephalus Magick in the Path of Dino Wicca

The Digital Gold Rush: Mastering E-Commerce and Online Sales

Future Shock: Adapting to the Next Decade of Change

The Quantum Mindset: Think Like a Billionaire

Sacred Motherhood: Awakening the Divine Feminine Within

The Mother's Spellbook: Enchantments for Love, Protection, and Prosperity

The Witch's Guide to Parenting: Raising Empowered and Intuitive Children

The Magick of Motherhood: Reclaiming Your Power Through Rituals

The Pagan Path to Self-Love: A Goddess's Guide to Worth and Confidence

Wild Woman Magick: Unleashing Your Primal Power

The Money Magnet Blueprint: Unlocking Unlimited Wealth

Biohacking 101: Unlock Your Body's Full Potential

The Wild Father: A Pagan Guide to Strength and Wisdom

The Sacred Masculine: Unlocking Your Inner Power

The Druid's Compass

The Warrior's Mindset

The Father's Fire

Odin's Path

Ancestral Bonds

The House That Whispers

The Magician's Code

The Wild Hunt

The Green Man's Path

The Altar of Success

The Shadow and the Sword

The High Priestess's Guide to Energy Healing

The Lunar Mother

The Sacred Self-Care Grimoire

The Womb Wisdom Codex

The Wheel of the Mother

The Witch's Guide to Manifestation

The Q2 Reset

The Ultimate Guide to AI-Powered Passive Income

Escape the 9-5

AI Feline Fortunes

The Tear-Stained Grimoire

Razorblade Runes
Cemetery Sirens
The Midnight Wristwatch
The Town That Forgets
AI Horror & Creepypasta
The Hollow Frequency
The Breach Echo
The Quiet Between Worlds
The Sigil of Tharan-Khul
Summon the Vault of Y'ha'ten
The Becoming Codex
The Profit of Az'ra-nar
The Drowned Logos
Echoes of the Eldritch Will
The Deep Ledger
Necronomicon of Networth
Covenant of the Wealthwyrm
The Whisperer's Manifesto
The Rites of Azh-K'luth
The Ark of the Crawling Coin
The Tithe of Shadows
Inkheart Abyss
The Timewinds of Y'ha-nthlei
The Spiral Labyrinth of Azag-Nirrh
The Gallifreyan Heresy of the Black Pharaoh
The Psalms of Nyog-Sotha
Black Rain Alchemy
The Infinite Maw
The Entropic Blueprint
The Oracle of Sh'guul
The Book of Breach
The Drowned Saint's Testament
Dreamcraft of the Sleeper God

The Silence Market
Cthonomics: The Dark Wealth Algorithm
Invocation of the Ten-Eyed King
Wealthbound to the Wyrm Below
Become the Unnameable
Codex of the Sovereign Flame
Rituals of Relentless Becoming
The Shadow Ascends
The Eyes Beneath You
The Will That Wakes Worlds
Silence Is a Weapon
The Mirror That Screams
The Whisper Between Moments
The Mind That Devours Fear
The Myth of the Finished Self
The Architect of Your Madness
The Voice You've Buried
The Discipline of Madness
Stormborn: Awakening Your Inner Tempest
The Mind That Ate Time
Unbind Your Becoming
The Pact You Owe Yourself
The Devourer's Diet
The Acid That Carves the Path
The Tower You Must Burn
The Breath Between Worlds
Speak Like the Deep
The Labyrinth Within
The Spine of the Sea God
Rejection Is a Portal
The Crown You Refused
The Scar Is the Spell
The Lightless Flame

The Habit of Becoming Horrific
ChickenJockey Chaos
The Gatekeeper Within
You Are Not Your Name
The Compass of the Mad
The Archive of Unsent Letters
What the Mirror Can't Show You
The Knife You Needed
Worship Nothing, Become Everything
The Other Voice
The Body the World Forgot
The Vein of the Void
The Black Bone Codex
The Puzzle of the Hidden Self (Millennium Puzzle)
The Eye That Sees the Lie *(Millennium Eye)*
The Ring of Return (Millennium Ring)
The Rod of Relentless Will ***(Millennium Rod)***
The Tally of the Soul (Millennium Tauk/Necklace)
The Key to the Locked Timeline (Millennium Key)
The Scale of Sacred Decisions (Millennium Scales)
Inferno Bites: The UnOfficial Minecraft Lava Cookbook
Rot in the Attic
Prana: The Hidden Force of Your Infinite Self
The Shadow Realm Within: Transforming Darkness Into Destiny
The Borderland Collapse
Claws of Protection: Bastet's Defensive Magick
Mr. Ring-a-Ding's Madness
Yugioh Astrology: Celestial Deckcraft and Duel Destiny (2026–2027 Edition)
The Seal You Signed: Unlocking the Power You Once Feared
The Puzzle of Infinite Minds: Unlocking the Mentalism Hidden Within

The Eye That Mirrors the All: Secrets of Inner Reflection
Doctor Who: The Toymaker's Broadcast
The Rod of Eternal Flow: Commanding the Currents of Vibration
Golden Eyes of Bastet: Enhancing Psychic Vision
The Key of Dual Forces: Balance Within the Polarity
The Scales of Living Rhythm: Timing the Dance of Life
The Necklace of Hidden Cause: Weaving the Webs of Fate
The Ring of Secret Masters: Rising Through the All Within All
Daggers of the Dying Deep
Bastet's Wealth and Fortune Magick: Prosperity Rituals of the Goddess
The Tide that Speaks
The Scrolls of Petosiris: 13 Rituals from the Feathered Eye
Petosiris and the Living Plague of Osirion
Feline Fire: Bastet's Passion and Love Magick
The Star Altar of Petosiris
Bastet's Whiskers: Supernatural Sensory Magick
The Bastet Grimoire
Feeding the Shadows
The Mouthless Prayer
The Spiral Wound
Becoming the Ibis: Lessons from Petosiris's Mind
The Crimson Coven: Cola Magick for Sweet Dominion
Sacred Cat's Paw
The Soda Zodiac: A Flavor for Every Sign
Covenant of the Crawling Flame
The Ink of Ish'Zur
Frothroot: The Thirst That Ate the World
The Golden Glyphs of Prosperity
The Etherbind Codex
Echoes of the Resistance: Reclaiming the You That Survived

Harnessed Minds: Breaking Free from Mental Control
The Eyes in the Smoke
Rootwake: The Carbon Covenant
Skitter Logic: Unlearning the Fear That Built You
Doctor Who: The World That Froths
Rootwake: The Fizz That Rewrites Flesh
Rootwake: Frothfather of the World
The Holly Pact: Blood Beneath the Mistletoe
The 2nd Mass Principle: Building Unbreakable Tribes
Web of Wits: A Survival Guide to Encounters with Anasi the Spider (Aunt Nancy)
The Hexbreaking Handbook: Effective Spells to Remove Curses
Pop Alchemy: Transform Your Life One Sip at a Time
The Mason Code: Leading in Unleadable Times
Petosiris and the Fifth Chamber of Thoth
The Ether Seed Within
The Parent of Tomorrow
Petosiris's Pyramid of Perpetual Wealth
Unlearn the World
Grimoire of the Hollow Tongue
Zodiac Weeds: Finding Your Strain Through the Stars
Aquarius Rises in the Bank
The Sugar God's Smile
The Skinclock Reversal: Biohacking the Face of Time
Debtburn: How to Obliterate What You Owe Forever
The Ice Cream Oracle: What Your Cone Says About Your Future
Silence Is Sovereignty: The Power of Being Unreadable
The Wind That Whispers Through Stone
Path of the Four Directions
Doctor Who: The Maestro's Symphony of Endings
Oxygen Grail: Breathing to Undo the Clock

Zodiacal Collapse: When Stars Devour Time

Teachings from the Red Sand Silence

Doctor Who: Omega – The Broken Equation

Memory Wipe Your Past: Start Over Like a MiB

Mitochondria Prime: Ignite the Core of Youth

A Nest of Roaches

Grub from the Galaxy: MiB Recipes You'll Never Forget

Whiskers of Power: Bastet's Guide to Inner Sovereignty

The Gift Must Cost Them: Negotiation Through Unequal Exchange

The Worm Guys' Wealth Code: Hustle Like an Alien

Bug Out: The Edgar Method for Ruthless Goal Setting

Weaving Life with Spiderwoman's Pattern

Doctor Who: The Rani's Renaissance

How to Get a Job (If You're a Puppygirl)

Speak Through Others: The Art of Proxy Power

T-Rex Your Trauma: Reclaim the Power of Your Primal Self

The Black Briefcase: How MiB Stay Wealthy in Silence

The Thirst Beyond Reason: Understanding Diabetes Insipidus From the Inside Out

Backwoods Witchcraft for Billionaires: The Pagan Path from Dirt Roads to Gold Roads

The Moonshine Grimoire: Fermented Spells for Abundance

The Nameless Geometry

The Wraith's Mixtape: Spellcasting with Songs of Sorrow

The Gallifreyan Gentleman: Silent Wealth, Sonic Confidence, and the Doctor's Code of Living

Sugar Water Confidence

Dino Totems: Spirit Guides from Earth's First Gods

Pumpkin Sigils & Ritual Smoke

The Hózhó Compass

The Distortus Discipline – Order from Inner Mutation

Witchcraft for the Cold-Blooded Soul

Moonlight Over the Blessingway
Water, Interrupted: When the Body Forgets How to Hold On
Deformed but Divine: Embracing Your Asymmetry
Hexes in the Henhouse: The Farm Witch's Guide to Power
The Reversed Flame: A Grimoire of Inverted Power
Salt, Cells, and Sanity: Reclaiming Balance with Diabetes Insipidus
King of the Broken: Crowning the Flawed Self
Moonlight Scars: Emo Moon Magick and the Art of Lunar Sorrow
Noose Spells: Magick of the Hanging Rope
The Goth Cathedral: Rituals of the Broken and Beautiful
The Cretaceous Codex: Dino Spirits and Fossil Magick
The Turkey Bones Ritual
Nine Lives of Manifestation: Unlocking Bastet's Reality Codes
Chaos Muscles: Building Strength from Twisted Pain
Emo Blood Magick: The Veins of Power
The 3AM Flood: Nighttime Urination, Sleep Loss, and the DI Spiral
The Silence Between the Stars
The Lemon Method: Sour Your Way to Success
Starlit Sovereign
The Rite of Twelve Gates: Walking the Gates of the Duat.
Cornbread and Conjure: Recipes for Riches and Rootwork
The Black Rose Rituals: Emo Love Spells and Obsession Magick
The Eternal Goodbye: Death Magick and Rebirth Rituals
Sinkrot: The Drain That Remembers
The Hybrid Mindset: Thinking Beyond Evolution
Bone Dry: Navigating Dehydration Before It Breaks You
Wreathcraft: Winter Sigils and Yuletide Spells
The Rite of Twelve Mouths

S'mores of the Damned: Haunted Recipes for Halloween Night

Rethink the Drink: A Beverage Survival Guide for DI Warriors

The Shadow Chord: Guitar Magick and Sonic

Malformed Yet Majestic: Leading When You Feel Wrong Inside

The Cursed Diary: Ink-Stained Spells of the Emo Soul

Anxiety Off Switch: Emergency Reset for a Fried Nervous System

The Energy Heist: How to Take Back Your Life from Drainers

Beyond the Bathroom: Rebuilding Your Social Life With DI

Coyote's Gift for Decision Makers

Ghoul-Goo: Spooky S'mores You'll Die For

Echoes in the Mirror: Scrying and Self-Destruction Magick

Thread and Thorn: Stitching Spells from Rural Cloth

The Mogwai Mind: Building Untouchable Wealth from Small Ideas

Be Your Own Guide: Trust Your Inner Compass

Hormones in Chaos: The Endocrine Puzzle of Diabetes Insipidus

ChronoCleanse: Detox Your Biological Timeline

The Limb You Hide Is the One That Saves You

Leaves, Bones, and Whisper Spells

The Dinosaur Mindset: Prehistoric Tactics for Modern Wealth

Clawing Back Control: A Bastet Method for Boundaries and Empowerment

Samhain Codes of the Forgotten

Orange Alchemy: The Autumnal Spellbook

Monster Within, Master Without

The Sigil That Sleeps

Hearthcraft: Yule Hearth Sigils and Winter Warmth Spells

Temple of the Purring Moon: Rituals from Bastet's Lineage
When the Earth Remembers Your Footsteps
Food for Mood: Eat to Heal Depression, Not Just Survive It
Witch of the Kudzu Vine: Southern Pagan Wealth Secrets
The Invisible Diagnosis: Advocating for Yourself With DI
The Coffin's Lullaby: Sleep Magick and Nightmares as Portals
Ashes of the Will: Rituals for Erasing the Self
The Fracture Rite: Shattering the Magickal Core
Funeral Candles: The Art of Emo Flame Magick
The Black Grimoire: A Blank Ritual for Writing in Absence
Phantom Thirst: A Halloween Survival Guide for Diabetes Insipidus
The Hollow Crown: Emo Royalty and Magick of the Outcast King
Sandpainting for the Soul
Falling Into Balance: Using the Extra Hour to Recalibrate Life
100 Southern Superstitions That Still Work
The DI Child: A Parent's Guide to Raising Hydrated, Happy Kids
The Jungle of Shame: Escaping the Hidden Lab of Doubt
The Witch's Toast: S'mores Spells and Creepy Confections
The Hoodoo Pantry: Spells from the Mason Jar
The Immortal Fortune: Secret Wealth Lessons from Captain Jack Harkness
The Specter's Embrace: Magick for Channeling Ghostly Lovers
Grateful Waters: A Thanksgiving Survival Guide for Diabetes Insipidus
The Seizure Gospel
Harvestbind: Autumn Sigils and Samhain Spells
Doctor Who: The Algorithmic Awakening
Silent Nights, Steady Waters: A Christmas Survival Guide for Diabetes Insipidus

The Extra Hour Effect: How One Hour Can Transform Everything

Blade Between the Breaths

Running with the Mountain Shadows

Echoes of the Failed Experiment – Becoming a Living Legacy

Swamp Witches & River Ghosts: Real Southern Hauntings

Cornbread Prophecies: Magical Recipes from a Southern Table

Doctor Who: The Signal in the Star

Bloomcraft: Spring Sigils and Equinox Enchantments

Vanisher: How to Disappear from the Internet Without Losing Your Life

The Ultimate Christmas Cookie Cookbook

The Unbreakable Parent: How to Mentally Survive Raising Kids in a Broken World

Time Debt: How to Reclaim the Hours You Didn't Know You Lost

One Month, One Million: Unconventional Cash Creation Tactics

Doctor Who: The Cyber Conversion Protocol

Black Friday Frenzy: The Art of Finding Hidden Online Deals

The Grimoire Buried Under the Apple Tree

Digital Couponing Masterclass: Your Step-by-Step Guide to Black Friday Savings

The Fire Inside the Flint

Shadows on the Ceiling: The Emo Guide to Astral Magick

The Bone-Eaters Beneath Us

Black Friday Bundle Blueprint: Creating Irresistible Product Packages for Maximum Sales

Thirteen Nights of Unbinding

Doctor Who: Engines of Influence

Pumpkin Spice Alchemy: Recipes of Fire and Frost

When Raptor Met Rexy: Prehistoric Lessons in Wild Romance

Oblivion's Candle: Burn the Path Behind You

Campfire Curses and Chocolate: A Halloween S'mores Grimoire

The Wallet That Wasn't Mine: Breaking Free from Inherited Scarcity

The Cola Zodiac: What Your Fizz Says About Your Fate

Frostfire Fortune: Unlocking Winter's Hidden Prosperity

Signal Jamming: Detox Your Brain from Info Overload

The Dust of the Forgotten Rite

The Golden Cat Sigils: Drawing Power in Bastet's Name

Mud Magick: The Prosperity of Getting Dirty

Savory Spicefall: Beyond the Pumpkin Pie

Pumpkin Spice Apothecary Kitchen

The Pumpkin Spice Economy: Turning Trends into Billions

The Ember Veil: 13 Nights of Fire Magick

Financial Freeze: When Earning Triggers Panic

The Gingerbread Alchemist: Sweet Recipes with a Twist

Biosynth Power: Programming Yourself from Scratch

Echoes from the Talking Circle

Truffle Alchemy: Fungus of Fortune

Spores of Power: The Truffle Witch's Handbook

Doctor Who: The Tower That Speaks

The Mycelium Veil: Truffle Magick Unbound

Broke But Ashamed: Healing the Shame Wound of Debt

The Evergreen Mind: Growth Through Winter Stillness

The Black Veil Truffle Rite

The Voice Beneath Symbols

Witchlight on the Bayou: Swamp Spells for Sovereignty

I Grew Up Poor and Now I Sabotage My Success

The Lantern of Hollow Souls

Shutdown Survival: A Citizen's Guide to Thriving When Government Stops

When Abundance Feels Like a Threat: Healing the Hidden Fears of Enough

The Scarecrow Grimoire

Owls of the October Veil

Candlewax and Curses: A Halloween Spellbook

Excavating the Inner Fossil – Transforming Fossilized Thoughtforms into Tools of Power

The Yule Witch's Spellbook: Magick for the Holiday Season

Haunted Christmas: Ghost Stories for Winter Nights

The Christmas Survival Guide: Thriving Through the Chaos

The Bone Orchard Rites

Haunted Commerce: The Ghost in the Marketplace

When Money Triggers the Inner Child

Silent Night with the Silence: A Christmas Thriller

The Lightning Crown: Living and Leading Through Seizures

TARDIS Tidings: Festive Stories from the Whoniverse

Autumn Reset: Slowing Down Without Falling Behind

The Trillion Dollar Soul: Rewriting the Currency of Reality

Truffle Eclipse Magick

Micro-Manifestations: Quick Magick That Works

5-Minute Rituals for Busy Witches

The Marshmallow Massacre: Halloween Treats with a Sinister Twist

Blood and Blackberry Thorns

Magickal Mornings: Rituals for a Blessed Christmas Day

Embers of the All-Hallows Fire

The Pumpkin Market Collapse

The Hour You Gained: Transforming Time Into Power

The Chamber Must Be Sealed: Mastering the Power of Controlled Access

The Cursed Manuscript of Petosiris

The Festive Hearth: Creating Holiday Traditions

Darkness Rising: Thriving as Nights Grow Longer

Harvesting Time: Turning the Year's End Into Your New Beginning

Petosiris and the 13th Zodiac Key

Wagewound: When Paychecks Become Identity Prisons

Walls That Watch

The Silent Feast: Rituals of Power in the Longest Night

The Distortus Legacy : Becoming a Deformed King in a Perfect World

The Hollow Masks

The Gratitude Furnace: Forging Gold from Thanks

Feast of Inner Gold: Eating for Energy and Enlightenment

Haunted Commerce: The Season of Spending Spirits

Fear Bonds: How Panic Creates Profit

Black Friday E-Commerce Playbook: Sales Tactics to Skyrocket Your Holiday Revenue

Budgeting for Black Friday: A Holiday Savings Planner

Haunting the Harvest Moon

The Warrior's Water: Emergency Preparedness for People With DI

The First Sip of the Year: A New Year's Survival Guide for Diabetes Insipidus

Doctor Who: The Thirteenth Node

The Unseen Struggle: Mental Health, Anxiety, and Chronic Thirst

The Hearth's Hidden Ledger: Counting Energies as Currency

The Gift Alchemist: Turning Any Offering Into Gold

The Papyrus of the Bound Spirit

The Magick of Leftovers: Transmutation in the Fridge

Frost and Fortune: Christmas Wealthcraft for the Modern Magus

Last-Minute Gifts: Creative Ideas on a Budget

10 Secrets to Surviving Holiday Crowds
The Witch's Dow Jones
The Witches' Graveyard Shift
Pumpkin Sigils: Carving Rites for Midnight Power
The Secret Shopper's Black Friday Guide: How to Get Early Access and VIP Deals
Fever in the Foundation
The Neuralyzer Reset: Reprogram Your Morning Routine
Lightning Lessons of the White Painted Woman
The Enchanted Snowflake
The Magic Sip: Surviving Disney Parks with Diabetes Insipidus
The One Who Draws Through You
Santa's Secrets: A Magical Holiday Planner
Silent Bells, Loud Miracles: Self-Help for the Season of Stillness
The Sugar Spell Codex: Confectionary Magick of Christmas
Autumn Hexcraft: Fallen Leaves, Fallen Barriers
Sleep Like a Fortress: Build a Life Where Insomnia Can't Survive
Nowhere Was Ever Home
Christmas Under the Stars: A Celestial Holiday Guide
Rentproof: How to Never Be Evicted Again
Workless: Escape the 9-5 Without Being Broke
The Gilded Gift: A Wealth Altar for Christmas Morning
The Black Friday Grimoire
The Hollowing: Ceremonies of Spiritual Collapse
Doctor Who: The Nameless Signal
Where the Eagle Hides His Courage
The Dwarf Tyrant's Ascent: Claiming Power in a World of Giants
The Currency of the Dead: Trading with Spectral Bankers
The Icebound Witch: Survival and Magick in the Cold

The Emergency Money Mind: Constant Crisis, Zero Calm

Thirst & Roses: A Valentine's Survival Guide for Diabetes Insipidus

Springing Into Clarity: Mastering the Energy Shift of Daylight Saving

Speed of the Nanotyrant: Agile Strategies for Life's Hunt

The 90-Day Reset: A Science-Backed Guide to Reinvent Yourself Before the New Year

The Coil of Thorns

Timegates Unleashed

Dopamine Fasting 2.0: Rewiring Your Brain in a World of Overstimulation

The Nanotyrannus Mutation: Embracing Your Differentiated Form

Unwritten January: How to Use the Blank Page of the Year to Re-Author Your Life

Feast of the Forgotten Spirits: Ancestor Magick for the Holidays

The Burnout Codex: A System for Thriving Beyond Stress

I Don't Deserve to Have Money

When the King Doesn't See You: The Shadow Predator's Guide

The Reset Ritual :A Guide to Shedding Last Year's Weight—Emotional and Physical—by Spring Cleaning Your Soul

Calendar Alchemy: Learn to Bend Time and Productivity around Your Natural Rhythms

The Mirror Contract: A One-Sentence Agreement with Yourself that Unlocks Real Change

The Nile Formula: Sacred Flow for Millionaire Minds

Forward Momentum: Productivity Rituals for the Lost Hour

Harvest Gold: Wealth Magick of Pumpkin Spice Commerce

The Magick of Christmas Lights: Illuminating Holiday Rituals

Cranberry Crown: Royal Self-Worth through Ritual Meals

Petosiris and the Worms of the Feathered Throne

The Evergreen Equation: Self-Help for Sustained Growth

The Rain Will Wash Us Away: Emo Weather Magick

Snowlight Shadows: Magick Under Frozen Stars

Doctor Who: Merger of Empires

The Light Within the Feast: Magickal Wealth of Yuletide Flame

Momentum Machines: Small Habits Designed to Snowball into Unstoppable Forward Motion

Calm Spells: Magickal Solutions for Anxiety Relief

Santa's Final List: The Naughty Never Leave

The Mystic's Guide to Banishing Worry

The Silence Dividend: Turning Quiet Mornings into Compounding Growth All Year

Charmed Stillness: Rituals to Ease the Mind

Blood Spiral Ascension

The Vanishing Heart Invocation

Crystal Calm: Harnessing Stones for Anxiety

The Nano Tyrant Code: Strength in the Small Predator

The Energy Ledger: Accounting Methods for Vitality, Not Just Money

Snowglobe Mindset: Shake Up Your Thoughts, Settle Into Peace

The Weight of the Feather: Anubis's Codes for Soul Balance

Pocket Peppermint Power: Tiny Rituals for Big Holiday Energy

Shadowkeeper of the Golden Jackal: Anubis's Path to Energetic Protection

The Witch's Breath: Anxiety Relief Through Magickal Breathing

The Tiny Ember: Pocket Motivation for Cold Days

The Twelfth Doctor: The Rebel with a Cause (Peter Capaldi, 2013–2017)

The Thirteenth Doctor: Breaking the Mold
(Jodie Whittaker, 2017–2022)

The Fourteenth Doctor: A New Beginning (David Tennant, 2022–2023)

The Fifteenth Doctor: Rewriting the Stars
(Ncuti Gatwa, 2023–2025)

Santa's Shortcut to Success: Micro Habits for a Better New Year

The Midnight Cocoa Manifesto: Comfort Rituals for Hard Nights

Why I Can't Save: Trauma Blocks to Financial Planning

Dino Brain, Mega Goals: Rewire Yourself for Savage Success.

Jurassic Profit: Unearth Your Inner Millionaire Fossil

Scales & Softness: Dating with Dino Heart

Carnotaurus Dreams.

Red Willow Thinking.

Reindeer Resilience: How to Keep Going When You're Exhausted

Candlewick Courage: Lighting Strength in Dark Seasons.

Elf-Mode Focus: Fast Attention Fixes for Busy Seasons

Futureproof Feelings: Emotional Skill-Building for Resilience No Matter What the New Year Brings

The 90-Day Rewire: Transform Your Neural Pathways Before Spring Blooms

Jolly Rich: Christmas Micro-Money Magick for Fast Prosperity.

Gingerbread Gratitude: Mini Practices for a Happier Holiday

Trauma-Spending: When Money Becomes a Drug

Goal Skeletons: Build Minimalist Frameworks for Resolutions That Last

The Snarl Strategy: Growling Back at a World That Silenced You

The Hourglass Reset: Reclaiming What the Clock Took

Yule Claw: Dino Rites of Light in the Darkness

Sacred Circles: Grounding Rituals for Anxious Souls

Clockstopper's Gut: Rebuilding the Core of Time

Winterfire Drive: Harness the Cold Season's Stillness to Ignite Deep Motivation

The 5-Minute Productivity Hack: Small Steps to Big Results

Light Ascending: A Self-Help Guide to Longer Days

Inner Economy: Trade Self-Doubt for Confidence Like a High-Value Currency

Simple Success: Decluttering Your Life for Better Results

The Resilient Mind: Thriving in Tough Times

The 2026 Playbook: Mastering the Year Ahead

The Spring Sleep Solution: Conquering Fatigue After Time Change.

The Hormonal Compass: Navigate Back to Your Youth

Golden Vision: Eating for Your Eye Color with the Power of Ghee

Lionhearted Love: Strength in Relationships

MiB Mindset: Think Like a Cosmic Agent

The Ladder of Small Wins: Climb Out of Stagnation by Stacking Micro-Victories

The Momentum Hour: Gaining More in Less Time.

The Year of You: A Self-Help Blueprint for Unapologetic Self-Ownership

The Dust That Watches You Back.

The Astral Parent

Shadow of the King: The Nanotyrannus Parable

Tiny Tidings of Triumph: Small Wins That Change Your Life

Dwarf Tyrant Rising: When You're the One They Overlook

The Bank Account Mirror: Healing How You See Yourself Through Money

Cretaceous Black

When Love Costs Too Much: Romantic Triggers and Financial Wounds

Dream-Eater's Guide to Wealth

Unzipped Reality: The Jacket That Opens Portals

The Power of No: How to Set Boundaries and Get Rich

Keeper of the Desert Veil: Anubis's Teachings on Illusion & Truth

Redacted Stargates: Stories the SGC Buried

The Clock That Dripped Time

Doctor Who: The Silent Acquisition

Hairline Manifestation: Unlocking Power at the Edge of Thought

Cash-Eater Crickets: How Insects Predict Economic Collapse

Dead Pet Whisperer: Grief Alchemy from the Other Side

The Love Algorithm Is Broken: Hack Romance Before It Hacks You

The Rite of the 8-Limbed Seal

Melt the Moon: A Fire Ritual to Reshape Emotion

Venomous Miracles: Healing Through the Poison Path

Wealth Without Water: The Post-Aquatic Rich Life

The Butterfly Betrayal: When Change Turns on You

The Quiet Upgrade: How Humans Are Secretly Rebuilding Themselves Without Asking Permission

Nobody Taught Us This: The Missing Human Manual for Money, Energy, and Self-Respect

You Were Never Broken: Why Most People Are Reacting Normally to an Unstable World

After the Noise Ends: How Humans Reset When the World Finally Goes Quiet

Burrowing into History: Groundhog Day Through the Ages
The Shadow Forecast: The Science of Groundhog Day
Choice Cascades: How One Decision in January Sets Ripples for the Whole Year
The Anti-Anxiety Blueprint: Mastering Fear and Stress for Success
The Ancestral Path of the Jackal Priest
Winterborn Titans: Giants of Ice and Stone
The Extinction Spire
The Emotion That Made Me Millions
Delete Their Voice: Become Unreachable
The Frostbound Mysteries: Mythical Beings of January's Chill
The Roar Within: Unlocking Your Potential
From Burrow to Sky: Groundhog Day Explained
The Boogey Book: Festive Ward-Off Edition
Fooled Ya! The Psychology Behind Great Pranks
April Fools' Alchemy: Transforming Everyday Items into Pranks
Anchor Habits: Root Yourself in Unshakable Routines That Endure Seasonal Change
Emerald Waters: A St. Patrick's Day Survival Guide for Diabetes Insipidus
The Groundhog's Legacy: Myths, Legends, and Facts
Six Weeks of Mystery: The Truth Behind Groundhog Day
The Upgrade Mind: Tech-Like Patches and Updates for Your Mental Operating System
Moon Blood, Star Flesh: Embracing Your Hybrid Nature
Groundhog Lore and Legend: A Complete Guide
You Are the Lie They Can't Kill
Download a Different Reality
The Quiet Advantage: Winning Without Announcing Yourself
A Year of Gratitude: Unlocking Joy

Touch Grass: A Pagan Reset for a Burned-Out Digital World

Cold Start Wealth: Building Financial Power from a Standing Still Point

Astrology Without Fate: Using Cycles Without Surrendering Control

The Future is Remote: Work Less, Earn More, Live Anywhere

Harvest of Silence

The Algorithm Knows Your Name

April Fools' Day for Introverts

Soft Power Systems: Influence That Doesn't Exhaust You

Practical Magick for Real Life: Focus, Intent, and Follow-Through

January Is a Lie: Designing Momentum Without the Calendar

Universal Flow: Managing DI in High-Energy Theme Parks

Electric Allure: Exploring Erotic Electro-Play

The Masked Embrace: Exploring Sensory Deprivation

The Ultimate April Fools' Survival Guide

Splashproof Survival: Waterparks & Wave Pools with DI

Agile Predator, Still King: Crafting Your Speed in a World That Celebrates Size

The Shadow Feast: Groundhog Day's Sinister Side

The Bug's Business Model

Edge of Bliss: Mastering the Art of Tease and Denial

Midnight Alchemy: Rituals for Transformation Between the Old Year and the New

Punxsutawney Bloodlines: A Groundhog Day Horror

The Burrower: Groundhog Day's Darkest Secrets

Buried Alive: A Groundhog Day Horror Story

Blood Moon Markets: The Witch's Guide to Wealth Magick

The Groundhog's Shadow: What It Means for the World

Seasonal Shadows: The Groundhog Day Phenomenon

The Shadow's Curse: A Groundhog Day Horror Tale

Punxsutawney Revealed: A Guide to Groundhog Day

Safari Hydration: Zoo & Wildlife Park Survival for DI
The Foolproof Prank Planner
Latex Lust: Embracing Fetish Fashion **is a sophisticated**
Whip & Whisper: The Dynamics of Impact Play
The Shadow Burrow Chronicles: Horror Beneath the Ground
Frozen Shadows: A Groundhog Day Thriller
The Groundhog's Revenge: A February Nightmare
Burrow of the Damned
Everyday Enchantment: Magickal Practices for Modern Living
Budget Bliss: The Easy Path to Financial Freedom
Six More Weeks of Terror
The Oxygen Debt
The Ice Veil: Mystical Beasts of January's Shadows
Roots That Remember
Polar Myths: Creatures of the Icy Abyss
The Marginalia Covenant
AI and the Occult: Digital Spirits, Sigils, and Cyber-Witchcraft
Roleplay Realms: Crafting Fantasies and Scenes
The Last Clean River
Lover in the Shadows: A Groundhog Day Tale
Buried Hearts: A Groundhog Day Gothic Romance
Anubis Wept for Petosiris
The Lantern Knows Your Name
Rituals of the Last Shadow
The Bell That Rings for No One
Shadows of Love and Death
The Groundhog's Bride: A Dark Valentine's Tale
Frozen Kisses: A Horror Romance for Groundhog Day
The Creative Spark: Igniting Your Passion Projects
From Cub to King: A Journey of Transformation
Six Weeks to Midnight: A Groundhog Day Romance
Tide of the Unclean

Burrow of Desire: A Groundhog Day Paranormal Romance

The Shadow Magick Almanac: Harnessing Groundhog Day Energies

AI for Emo Influencers: Growing an Online Following Without the Anxiety

AI for the Melancholy Millionaire: Making Money Without Social Interaction

Winter's Grip: A Horror Romance Beneath the Frost

Shadowed Hearts: A Love Buried in Winter's Chill

The Shadow Lover: A Groundhog Day Gothic Love Story

Beneath the Burrow: A Groundhog Day Thriller

The Punxsutawney Conspiracy

The Crimson Pact: Emo Blood Oath Magick

The Shadows of Gallifrey: A Doctor Who Horror Collection

Whispers in the Vortex: Chilling Tales from the TARDIS

AI Ghostwriting for Emo Souls: How to Make Money Writing Without Trying

The Anti-Social Emo's Guide to AI-Powered Freelancing

Emo AI Therapy: Talking to Robots When Humans Suck

Cry & Collect: AI-Powered Passive Income for Emos

The Weeping Angel Chronicles: A Collection of Terror

Dating Without the Mask

The Clockwork Menace: Horror Stories from the Future

Tender Doesn't Mean Weak

Not a Burden, Not a Bonus

Dalek Nightmares: Stories of Ultimate Extermination

The Empty Child's Curse: Tales of Horror and Fear

The TARDIS Ghost Files: Hauntings Across the Universe

Soft Armor, Open Heart

Chosen Gently

Love That Doesn't Rush You

Financial Gaslighting: When You're Made to Feel Crazy About Money.

After the Bees Went Silent

The Soil Knows Your Name

The Quantum Magick Codex: Unlocking the Hidden Laws of Reality

The Gingerbread Golem's Awakening: A Tale of Sweet Revenge

The Gingerbread Golem Chronicles: Guardians of Frost Hollow

The Power of Focus: Eliminate Distractions, Achieve Greatness

Sacred Submission: The Dynamics of D/s Relationships

The Magick of Numbers: Unlocking the Hidden Codes of the Universe

Blood and Bones: The Ancient Magick of Life and Death

Doctor Who: The Collapse Dividend

Thesis of the Unremembered

Desired as You Are

The Energy Budget of Love

Romancing Your Potential: The Love Month Growth Guide

Seen, Not Studied

Screams from the Void: Horror Stories Inspired by Doctor Who

The Silence Is Watching: A Collection of Dread

Under the Floorboards

The House of Feathers and Fangs

Emperor Bones, Hollow Crown

Goreglyphs of the Boiling Deep

The Coven That Screamed Back

The Stacks That Breathe

Love That Adapts

Nightmares on Gallifrey: Frights from the Doctor Who Universe

Apache Ways to Heal Powerfully

The Collector's First Lesson
Glyph Failure Syndrome
Philip Wittebane and the Discipline of Lies
The Making of Belos
Flesh Does Not Belong
The Golden Guard Prototypes
Coven Marks as Control Wounds
The Voice Belos Invented
The Boogeyman Within: Shadow Work for Personal Transformation
The Energy Edge: Reclaiming Your Power
Mindful March: A Quick Guide to Intentional Living
Love on Autopilot: Rekindle Your Relationship Instantly
Spring Renewal: Refresh Your Mindset Before the Equinox
Velvet Control: The Subtle Art of Erotic Choking
Erotic Shadows: Playing with Voyeurism and Exhibitionism
The Green Pulse Awakens
Equinox Bones
Immortality Is a Disease
Cold-Blooded Focus
The Invasive Advantage
The Lonely Assassin's Love: A Weeping Angel Romance
Philip Is Still Inside
Become the Signal That Replaces the Noise
When the Soil Says Yes
Shedding What No Longer Protects You
The Shadow Key: Unlocking the Power of Your Dark Self
The Enchanted Chocolate Rituals: Magickal Recipes for Love & Wealth
Love in the Vortex: A Doctor Who Horror Romance
Grimwalker Number Seventeen
The Boy Who Woke Again

Sad Girls Don't Beg: Reclaiming Self-Worth When Melancholy Is Mistaken for Weakness
Raising Pagan Children in a Non-Pagan World
The Pagan Homeschool Exit Strategy
Protecting Childhood While Preparing for Adulthood
Curriculum for the Dead
Too Much for Who? Reclaiming the Power of Intensity
Your Nervous System Is the Algorithm
Memories That Don't Belong to Him
The Golden Guard Template
Time-Locked Hearts: A Gallifreyan Gothic Romance
Ostara's Hatchlings: Fertile Dino Magick
The Dalek's Heart: A Tale of Forbidden Love
The Jackal's Final Game
Where Wild Magic Took My Brother
Where Love Meets Reality
Volume Without Apology
The Mind of Stillness: Petosiris's Hidden Teachings on Power
Doctor Who: The Final Shareholder Meeting
The Archive of Unfinished Lives
AI for Emo Musicians: Automating Your Sad Soundtracks
AI-Generated Emo Art: Selling Melancholy in Digital Form
Ashes Where the Cathedral Slept
The Monarch of Splintered Wings
People-Pleasing Is a Survival Strategy Past Its Expiration Date
Velvet Carnage Covenant
The Intensity Advantage
Attention Is a Finite Resource—You're Overspending It
Emotional Debt Compounds Faster Than Money
The Siege of Thornlit Graves
When the Bone King Wept Black
Comfort Is the Most Expensive Addiction

The AI Gothpreneur: Building a Business Without Any Social Interaction

AI & Tarot: Emo Divination for the Digital Age

Sad AI Aesthetics: Emo Branding & Personal Style

Black Sails Over a Dying Sun

The Crimson Parliament of Wolves

Cathedral of Veins and Thunder

The Orchard of Hanging Saints

The Self-Discovery Path: Find Your True Purpose

You Were Taught to Self-Sabotage Politely

Chrysalis Debt: Reborn into Wealth

Empire of Teeth and Perfume

The Devourer's Bride of Iron Mist

The Dormitory with No Windows

Built Larger Than the Room

The Silence Between Wings

The Manuscript That Grades You

The Librarian Who Refused to Die

Footnotes for a Burning Campus

The Thornblood Accord

The Paranormal Files: True Encounters with Ghosts, Aliens, and the Unexplained

Warfare in the Temple of Shattered Constellations

The Crow's Codex: Unlocking the Secrets of the Black-Winged Messengers

Purring Boundaries: Bastet's Guide to Raising Fierce Children

The Arcane Wealth Formula: Spellcasting for Infinite Abundance

The Celestial Spellbook: Harnessing Planetary Magick for Power and Fortune

Silk Shrouds of the Frostbound Wilds

Windtalker: The Hill Witch's Guide to Whisper Magick

The Doctrine of Psyence: Knowledge Beyond the Veil

The Bone Sovereign's Final War Chant

The Abyssal Altar of Salt and Silver

The Lantern Wilds That Devoured Lovers

The Court of the Sable Scar

Wax & Whispers: The Art of Candle Play

The Billionaire's Blueprint: Unlocking Wealth Through Action

The Cleansing Flow: Unlocking Wellness with Enema Therapy

Seasonal Gratitude: How to Thrive Before Spring

Beyond the Closet Door: Unlocking Your Full Potential by Embracing Fear

The War-Bound Crown

Eternity With Teeth

The Observer Is the Spell: Reality as Psychic Architecture

Mis-Classified Monster: Redefine Yourself

Claws Without Cruelty: The Bastet Discipline Method

Claws Without Cruelty: The Bastet Discipline Method

Temple Mothers: Parenting in the Spirit of the Sacred Cat

The Sixth Extinction You Can Stop

Ticket to the Unseen

The Basement Doesn't Stay Shut

Exhibit of Moving Bones

The Creek That Brings Things Back

No-Exit Hallway

The Tourist Who Knew Their Names

The Limestone Choir

The Room That Remembers Pain

Briar Hollow's Missing Hour

The Gift Shop of Cursed Souvenirs

The Stag in the Ceiling

Two Journals, One Lie

The Museum Eats Its Own Map
The Other Side Leaves Footprints
The Town That Forgets Faces
The Limestone Mouth
The Curator's Ledger of Regrets
The Portrait That Bleeds Tomorrow
The Visitor in Maeve's Voice
The Artifact That Wants to Be Worn
Briar Hollow's Second Sky
The Basement Opens in a Dream
Taxidermy That Isn't Dead
The Rift Key Wedding Ring
The Engine Under Limestone
The Town Under Pressure
Regret Is a Doorway
Boundary Law
The Bunker Beneath Briar Hollow
Concrete Cannot Keep It Out
Gravity Pockets
The Woman in the Static
The Rift Breathes.
Bone of the Threshold
The Cost of Return
The First Crossing
The Woman Who Came Back Wrong
Tethered Heart
The Heir Clause
Severance Geometry
The Witch's Shadow
After the Snap
THE LAND REMEMBERS
The Watchers in the Trees
Museum Under Surveillance

The Creek That Splits
The Line of Antlers
the beacon year
The First Wendigo Tracks
Hunger in the Pines
The Chupacabra Flock
Teeth in the Roof
Ghosts of the Overlap
The Double in the Creek
Forbidden Fruit: Kink and Food Play
Hydrocephalus and Mental Health
Flowing Well: Mindfulness Practices for Hydrocephalus
Managing Hydrocephalus: Tips for a Better Life
The Antler Choir
The Containment Year
Territory Marked
The County Line Fracture
The Night the Pines Bent
The Museum Command
The Threshold Proposal
The Stabilized Hour
The Rift That Watches Back
The Future That Split
The Forbidden Grimoire of Shadows: Unlocking Dark Magick's Hidden Secrets
The Witch's Code: Ancient Magick for the Modern Practitioner
The Antler Network
The Society of the Threshold
The Fracture Storm
Meditative Healing for Hydrocephalus
The Legacy Code: Creating a Life That Matters
The Rival Signal

The Night of Two Skies
The Eve of Vows
The Minimalist Path to Success
Wedding Under the Fractured Sky
The Visionary's Guide: Shaping Your Dream Life
Magick on a Budget: Making Your Dreams Come True
After the Silence
The Lone Cypress Grand
The Boogeyman Blueprint: Reprogramming Your Mind for Success
The Night Terror Method: Using Fear to Unlock Hidden Strength
The Boogeyman Paradox: Why Fear Is the Key to Success
Sleeping with the Boogeyman: How to Find Peace in the Darkness
The Velvet Invitation
Class of the Unprogrammed
The Fourfold Temptation
Diplomas for the Divine
The Collapse at Lone Cypress
The Anchor Strengthens
You Were Never Meant to Work
The Cracking States
Soft Voice, Sharp Will — How Introverted Goths Command Rooms Without Raising Their Tone
The Ceremony Was Always Within
Jurassic Shadows: The Return of the Prehistoric Plague
Carnivore Fog: A Mist of Terror
The Raptor's Curse: Blood of the Moon
Fossil Fury: Bones of the Dead
Predator Abyss: The Deep Below
The Geometry of Opposition
The Continental Choir

The Candle on the Porch: Hearth Spells of the Rural Rich

The Origin of Antlers

Cretaceous Crypt: Death Below the Ice

Terror Claws: The Pack That Hunts the Night

The Dino King's Wrath: Legends Reborn

Savage Earth: The Reign of the Raptors

Primal Terror: Jungle of the Lost

The Final Roar: Humanity's Last Stand

Time is Your Ally: Mastering Productivity with Ease

The Oak Knows Your Name: Forest Witch Wisdom for Wealth

The Rift Exodus

The Fractured Nation

The Coastal Shift

The Lunar Witch's Book of Spells: Moon Magick for Every Phase

Elemental Mastery: The Magick of Fire, Water, Air, and Earth

The Sorcerer's Almanac: Rituals and Spells for Every Season

The Magick of Words: Spells, Chants, and Enchantment for Power

The AI Dating Coach: How to Attract Love in the Digital Age

Boomstick Magick: Fire, Hunting, and the Spell of Sovereignty

www.ingramcontent.com/pod-product-compliance
Lightning Source LLC
LaVergne TN
LVHW020235210926
848481LV00016B/2217
* 9 7 9 8 3 4 9 2 1 5 4 1 4 *